GRILL COOKBOOK

FOR BEGINNERS

A Guide to Preparing Delicious and Healthy Foods over the Grill

ELBERT ROW

Table of contents

Introduction:

Cooking food on a grill over a heating source, such as ceramic briquettes or charcoal fire heated by gas fires, is classified as grilling. Direct heat easily sears the exterior of food, resulting in distinct robust, roasted, and sometimes surprisingly charred tastes as well as a good crust. When the meat is prepared over medium heat, it develops a crust and a smokier flavor. Grilling is something you are actually doing on the grill most often: rapidly preparing food over an intense fire at elevated temperatures. Grilling, in contrast to barbecuing, is warm and quick that gives food a simple sear. You are grilling whether you are cooking steak, seafood, hot dogs, hamburgers, pork chops, sausages, or chicken breasts without bones. Grilling fruits and vegetables are also common. Grilling at home is more usually performed on a charcoal grill. The words barbecuing and grilling are also used interchangeably. Barbecuing is the process of cooking food at a low temperature over an extended period of time. Meats such as mutton, poultry, pork, and turkey are slowly cooked at 225 degrees F or lower using this process.

Food that is grilled does not contain any extra fat. When you are grilling, the fats spill off the grates. Consider burgers cooked in the frying pan. Even as you move the meat to your dish, the fat pools mostly on a skillet. Furthermore, the fat is made on the grill. Meat that has been grilled retains more nutrients, including riboflavin and thiamin. Nutrients are important for good health. It also has nutrients that are close to those present in foods. Grilling burger patties is something that most people are familiar with. You should spice up the grilling menu. Choose the leanest beef for burger patties. Test the package and see if it says 93/7 on it. This constitutes just 7% of overall fat. You'll be happier if you consume leaner beef. Marinate the steaks of pork, ham, or beef. Honey garlic glaze, teriyaki sauce or salt and pepper are both options. Marinating these increases the spice as well as the wellbeing. In reality, marinating the meat helps to extract 99 percent of other chemicals.

Chapter 01: Basics of Grilling

This chapter gives detail about the grilling. What is grilling, which foods you can grill, and what are the health benefits of grilling food as well as withdraws are included in the chapter. How grilling actually works and how you can grill properly using some tips and tricks are also discussed in detail and depth. Differences between grilling and barbequing and some of the safety precautions of grilling food are also included in this chapter.

1.1 Understanding grilling

Grilling is defined as a quick, dry heat technique of cooking that employs a notable amount of radiant, direct heat, according to science. Active heat is used while cooking in a griddle, pan while thermal emission is used when grilling.

Grilling levels often reach 260° or 500°F, make this a quick-cooking process that must be closely watched. Otherwise, the freshly fried hot dogs can easily transform into path flares. Browning of sugars and proteins, meat as well as vegetables, which produces the magnificent color and additional flavor profile, is what really makes grill meals taste better. The reaction named Maillard occurs as foods exceed levels over 310 °F or 155 °C, and it induces browning. Actual grilling consists of preparing food through an open grid, with the flame either higher or lower of your food. Broiling is the word we use where the source of heat should be above, but that also comes within our concept of grilling.

Differentiation of grilling and barbecuing:

Grilling: The bulk of people cook dinner in the backyards. When many of us mention barbecue, we are talking about this. Grilling is the practice of cooking foods rapidly and in a high-temperature setting. Typically, it's achieved over a high flame. Grilling is suitable for meats such as pork chops, steaks, hamburgers, seafood, and hot dogs. Cooking several fruits and vegetables, mostly on a grill, is also a pleasant idea. Grilling takes place over the heavy fire, which ensures the flame is directly under the beef.

Barbecuing: Barbecuing is the practice of preparing food steadily and slowly. Barbecuing is widely used for meat cuts such as pork shoulder, ribs, beef brisket, and whole chicken or turkeys. These meats are harder and require the medium, slow temperature of a bbq to become tender. Barbecued food is cooked for a long period at a very low temperature. Barbecuing is frequently performed using indirect flame, in which the heat supply is linked to the area in which the meat is placed, so the meat isn't really specifically over its flame, as is the case with a barbecue. The source of heat for a barbecue is normally wood or charcoal. Various forms of wood emit numerous smoky tastes, which the meat may consume. Best food chefs take pleasure in using a long period of cooking to produce the juiciest, aromatic beef.

1.2 How to grill properly?

Techniques for grilling:

These fundamentals can assist you with learning how and when to barbecue. Keep in mind the following guidelines:

- Enable too much time to set up and prepare the barbecue grill once you start cooking. Have an insight into what you're grilling at all times.

- To stop sticking, hold the grill surface clean.

- Get the requisite grilling equipment on board.

- Spray water bottles cannot be used to monitor flare-ups, so this would just cause the fire to severe. More fat and humidity trigger flare-ups. Trim any extra fat off any food you intend to cook ahead of time, then transfer the meat to a separate section of your grill as you flip it to clear out all the fat droplets.

- Spice your food at least an hour before you grill to allow the flavor to sink in.

- Oil your food, not your grill. At high temperatures oil burns away, so it is useless to oil the grate of cooking.

- Place grilled food on a clean plate, specifically when cooking raw meat.

- Do not put sweet sauces or marinades your meat on your grill since it causes burning on open fire.

- Keep the grill apart from anything that can easily burn like fences, lighter fluid, your house, etc.

How you can cook vegetables and meat using a grill

A grill can create a temperature which is high, enabling food to be cooked easily and thoroughly. Switch on the fire and prepare thin meats and small stuff like chicken wings, steaks, hot dogs and ribs fast. Because of the quick tempo, you must keep an insight on your grill and, most specifically, the cooking. After all, grilling all high and easy is not the route to go. Low temperature is better for grilling meat, chicken, fruits, and vegetables; strive for low heat for these items. This involves lowering the temperatures on the gas grill and making a bigger fire on a charcoal grill. While you can always keep an eye on these ingredients, they can require time to prepare at a very low temp.

Temperature setting while grilling:

That temperature knobs on the gas grill give a clear indicator of how much high flame or the low flame is. How then do you feel that moderate hot heat is if you have a barbecue grill? There exists a procedure for gauging temperature with only your palm. Keep the hand above just the cooking plate and count down the seconds before you can no longer bear the flame. The low the heat, the more you could maintain your hands just above flames. This process operates on both charcoal and gas burners. The below are the laws to follow:

- Five seconds for very low heat

- Three seconds for medium to high heat

- One second for Incredibly hot

- Four Seconds for Mild heat

- Two Seconds for Incredibly hot

Flipping food on your grill:

A popular grilling misconception is that grilled meats cannot be turned too often. You like cooking, so switch when appropriate. To stop flare-ups, shift the foods all over the flame to make use of the limited area. And do not be alarmed because beams are inevitable, particularly when consuming high-fat meals like steak.

How to grill using indirect heat?

Some food benefits from indirect heat cooking apart from the hot source. This ensures the food should be on the side of your grill while the fire is on the other. It's perfect for cooking big foods, including whole chicks, beef steaks, racks of rib, or any other meat or the meat that takes a long cooking period. Indirect grilling helps you to cook the protein through to the core until the exterior burns and if you have a wide barbecue with multiple burners, it's safer to position the meal in the center and flame the grills on both sides. Place the meat on each edge and flame the grill on another if your grill grate is too tiny for that kind of configuration. To cook a meal accurately, you'll need to move it.

How to know when the food is done

Although there are several basic grilling time rules, deciding when meat is ready may be challenging. These are three guidelines of grilling success:

Rule 1: Meat that isn't thoroughly cooked will destroy you.

Rule 2: You can prepare food for longer amounts of time but still can't uncook it.

Rule 3: Confidence and check. When it comes to cooking to the correct doneness, expertise is the ultimate tool that you have; however, a meat thermostat is needed to ensure you get it right.

Method of Gas grilling:

Regulation is still the most common advantage of such a gas burner. You can quickly change the temperature with the spin of a dial to bring it where ever you like it. Before using your grill, read the owner's manual and adopt these measures for a good grilling experience:

- Switch up the heat on control valves and illuminate that grill.

- Switch on a gas supply and protect your barbecue.

- Prepare the grill by preheating it. In around ten min, a decent grill must be hot.

- Enable that grill to cool entirely before reinstalling the cover.

- Put the meat mostly on a griddle pan and sit there until it heats. The food would cook fast if you quit, and you risk burning it.

- Cleaning the work surface with only a grill cleaner is a smart practice.

- Flip as required and delete when finished.

- Wash off the work surface with your grill cleaner.

- Enable that grill to heat up for a minute on warm.

- Switch off the power grid and the ignition valves.

Charcoal grilling:

In contrast to gas grilling, the grilling with charcoal is indeed a realistic art style. While it offers a more natural grilled taste and barbecue experience, it is not as simple or convenient as preparing on the gas burner. No temperature regulation valve remains on a barbecue grill, regardless of how costly it is. The manner you create a burn, change the vent and hold the cover on everything influences the temperature. It needs a bit more time and commitment to learning, but it's just as flexible as just a gas burner. Charcoal grilling may hit temperatures of over 700 degrees Fahrenheit or remain below 200 degrees Fahrenheit. Searing a steak when cooking it on low heat is possible. A rotisserie is an alternative to several charcoal grills.

Initiation of Charcoal grilling:

Sometimes grill and charcoal are not enough for effective charcoal grilling. When it comes to charcoal grilling, there are a few things to remember. Clean the charcoal grill; debris block and ashes vent and cause it impossible to manage the flames. Check the vents for usability; corroded or rusted vents are difficult to adjust. Have two fire-resistant gloves on hand. Be aware that charcoal grilling implies the handling of hot objects; be prepared. Using the charcoal starter or charcoal chimney to help illuminate the charcoal. Place the grill of charcoal in a secure location that will not be turned over. Grilling instruments should be kept near at hand. Move the burning coals about inside your grill with a grill tool or good stick. Practice it. Mastering charcoal grilling requires time, but its well worth it.

How to light the charcoal fire?

Building the charcoal flame requires practice. Here are some tips to get you to begin:

To start your fire, ignite your charcoal and then expand it out. It takes ten to fifteen minutes for charcoal to achieve the right temperature. As charcoal becomes ready to grill, it will be covered with smoke, look white, grey and hot. Spread the charcoal in such a thin layer upon its coal plate for a moderate burn. Light sufficient charcoal on a coal pit to build the dual coat of coals for a hot burn. Whenever the charcoal becomes ready, drive it all to one half of the coal pit and barbecue from another side of the pan for such an approximate burn.

1.3 Pros and cons of grilling

Pros:

Cook is faster:

It's difficult to equate gas grills to other types of cookware. This grill takes enough time to heat, allowing you to spend more time on other things. They need a small amount of time that some cooking techniques do.

This also helps you save money you might have spent rushing to a restaurant for a bite to eat. Grills cause heat to accumulate, resulting in a faster cooking phase. As opposed to the others, it has a faster ignition or heating rate.

Controllable temperature:

It can hit a stage when the heat is either too little or too high when grilling. And in gas burners, temperature regulation is simple and can be accomplished by turning a specific knob. Trying to control temperature on a charcoal barbecue, on the other hand, requires ample airflow. While it's not complicated, it's no substitute for the comfort of the knob. Temperature plays an important role while grilling. So before you carry a griller inside, make sure your knobs work. Using the replacement programs to have a new computer if they malfunction within a limited period.

It is economical:

Gas grills can be expensive to purchase at first. Then, you would soon discover that it's the most cost-effective alternative available in the area. Other types of grills are known for their low costs, which then became an issue due to the rising fuel prices. On the other hand, due to the low cost of petrol, grills of gas would remain inexpensive in the longer run. You will have sufficient money to purchase additional grilling items for the house.

Safe to use:

Except for grills of charcoal, which emit carbon emissions that can cause respiratory problems, gas grills seldom emit such fumes. And it doesn't have any garbage, such as ash that might be swept to the other buildings by the storm. Although there is less waste with gas grills, they do need your focus in the event of a mechanical malfunction.

Everything can be cooked by grilling:

Regulating the humidity and heat is key to successful cooking. It is something that grills of gas have, which means that you can prepare each meal to your own preferences. The low temperature on a barbecue grill requires time, which may result in certain foods being burned. The broad temperature range allows slow cooking, which results in healthier meals.

Usage is comfortable:

Charcoal grills come with a long list of labor requirements, starting with the purchase of fuel and lighting it. Surprisingly, the majority of people, particularly the young, have never used charcoal method. As a result, persuading certain citizens of the value of these grills becomes challenging. Regardless of how much stress you experience from the others, choose brands that you are familiar with and resist carbon in any way. Don't be misled by low prices; it might ultimately cost you a lot of money. Gas grills are easy, quick, and convenient to use. Unlike barbecue grillers, you do not have to do that from outside.

Grilling is healthy:

Foods cooked on the gas grills are reported as being low in fat. Fried items, unlike the grilled food, face a number of health hazards, including obesity and related disease. Surprisingly, even low-fat foods appear to increase in fat content when fried. Gas grillers have the advantage of sucking up extra fat, which is particularly useful for slow-cooking. As a result, fewer calories are consumed, resulting in a more stable weight.

Cons:

Most people consider grilling to be a pleasurable and relaxing activity. Grilling often contributes to the healthiness of the meals you prepare. In reality, only three out of four American families own a barbecue. Still, it is ingrained in our lives as Americans. However, it appears that grilling isn't quite simple or enjoyable, as some suggest. Grilling necessitates a great deal of effort, planning, and certain essential skills. Grilling can have additional drawbacks. There are a couple of aspects that may be considered a downside to grilling, depends on the viewpoint. If the burner becomes too hot, the food can be dried out quicker, and some grills may be dangerous to the atmosphere. Depending on what type of grill and how long it'll take for all the grill to heat up, grilling can take longer than normal cooking. In the end, you must consider when the flavor of the meal and the time required for the grill are worth that to you.

From the point of grilling:

Despite the fact that gas grills have many benefits over traditional grills of charcoal, people begin to use the latter despite their numerous drawbacks. To begin with, the method of grilling is only possible throughout the summertime. If you choose to barbecue in the other weather, indoors grilling may be a hassle and a mess since the roof and walls can blacken. Furthermore, the individual tasked with grilling will be unable to appreciate anything because this activity usually requires relentless focus. To avoid burning or charring, he will have to transform the meat regularly. It takes a long time and a lot of effort to get a charcoal grill up and running. You must heat your charcoal until it is almost white. Furthermore, smoking irritates your lungs and contaminates your meal, causing it toxic. It's almost as exhausting to clear up once you've finished grilling. Charcoal grills produce lots of smoke, which isn't the problem for the grills of gas. Soot accumulation on meat may also be caused by a lack of oxygen supply.

From the point of the environment:

Grilling on a barbecue grill is the conventional method. This provides us with delicious food, but it is very dangerous to the climate. We all know that burning charcoal produces soot and smoke, which pollutes the air we breathe and can damage the respiratory systems and eyes. Nobody enjoys seeing smoke in their eyes.

From the point of fitness:

Grilling, as previously said, generally requires certain fundamental skills. It is important to have a basic understanding of the devices you're dealing with. When grilling, it's simple to overcook. We can all agree that properly burned meat tastes great and has fewer calories, but this is not ideal for our well-being. Not in the least. We also understand that grills operate only at high temperatures. However, as the extreme heat of a grill comes into contact with proteins in the beef, several possible carcinogens form on the surface. Moreover, the marinades and fat that drips off the beef, through grates, onto the charcoal condense and vaporize on the food, imparting the smoky flavor. And did you notice that this delectable char is often very unhealthy? What is the reason for this? Because of the formation of the advanced glycation end the products, which may lead to asthma, cardiac disease, Alzheimer's disease, among other problems. Undercooked food is just as unhealthy as overcooked meat. Many times, the surface of the beef is perfectly crisped, and the inside is already unfinished. This kind of meal is very detrimental to one's well-being.

From the point of economic:

Gas grills have been very common in recent years. When opposed to charcoal grills, they are also easier to clean after use. A good gas grill will set you back around $300. As a result, even though it closes the void in your gut, it leaves a large one in your wallet. Infrared grills are the type of gas grill. They were selected as they have a clear fire, which allows your meat to be cooked quickly on a grill. However, because of the bulky weight, infrared grills remain costly and difficult to transport. And, the compact models aren't ideal for everyday usage or intimate gatherings. They also don't have a low-temperature control option. As a result, they can't be used to barbecue vegetables or fish.

1.4 Precautionary measures for grilling

Precautionary measures for the Gas grill:

- Apply a mild water and soap solution to the nozzle, which will release bubbles and expose any escaping gas.

- Per year, examine the cylinder of the gas nozzle for leakage when 1st time using.

- Turn the gas tank off and grill whenever you smell or expect a gas leak with no fire and if the gas leak ends, get it serviced by a specialist before again using it. If the leakage does not end, call the fire service.

- Gas grills and even propane tanks – should always be kept outdoors and out from your home.

- Do not turn the gas on when the lid is closed. The gas can ramp up inside, causing the lid to fly off and injure or burn people.

- When you smell smoke or gas when frying, move back from the grill and contact the fire service right away. Attempting to shift the grill is not a good idea.

- When you've done cooking, ensure that your gas grill's valve is fully closed.

Precautionary measures Charcoal grill:

- Examine metal grills for rust exposure, which may allow the charcoal to drop through the surfaces below and start a fire.

- When the kindling or coals have already been lit, don't apply charcoal starter fluid. To launch a fire, never use something combustible or flammable.

- After the fires have died out on a charcoal grill; it will stay hot for several hours. When coals are warm, avoid putting something flammable around the grill or pushing. Keep away flammable things from a grill that could be carried by the air.

- Be sure you have the right starter fluid on hand. Keep it out of the hands of children and out of direct sunlight.

- Do keep an eye on the grill.

- Rekindle the fire with more charcoal and dry kindling if necessary if it has died out. Liquid fuel may not be added since it can spark an intense fire.

Chapter 02: Breakfast, Desserts and Fruits

This chapter will help you to learn and experiment with the different basic varieties of recipes that are used on a daily basis in breakfast timing or as starters. It also includes some recipes for grilling fruits that can be used as deserts. It definitely consists of an infinite number of options to try according to your flavor.

2.1 Grilled Guacamole

Prep time: 10 mins

Cooking time: 20 mins

Servings: 8

Ingredients:

- Two avocados

- Two jalapeños

- Two unpeeled cloves of garlic

- Juice of one and a half limes

- Half chopped red onion

- One tomato, chopped and medium-sized

- A quarter cup of cilantro, chopped

Instructions:

Preheat grill over a medium heat halve avocados and place them on a preheated grill, along with garlic and jalapeños. Cook, until it turns brown. Now put this in a bowl and also add some garlic cloves with lemon juice. Mash avocado and clove of garlic together. Remove the stems from jalapeños and cut them. Sprinkle peppers and add to the bowl with avocado, along with cilantro and tomato. Season with the salt and stir to combine. Now, food is ready to serve.

2.2 Grilled Watermelon

Prep time: 10 mins

Cooking time: 15 mins

Servings: 5

Ingredients:

- ¼ cup of honey
- zest of 1 lime and juice
- One small watermelon
- Mint leaves freshly torn for serving
- One tablespoon of olive oil
- Sea salt, for serving

Instructions:

Heat your grill or grill pan to medium heat. Stir, together zest lime and juice, olive oil, and honey. Then, spray lime juice mixture all over the watermelon wedges and place them on the grill. Cook for around 2 minutes per side until the fruit softens slightly. Sprinkle some mint and flaky sea salt. Serve your food immediately.

2.3 Grilled Peaches

Prep time: 5 mins

Cooking time: 10 mins

Servings: 4

Ingredients:

- Halved and pitted four ripe peaches
- One tablespoon of canola or vegetable oil
- Vanilla ice cream, for serving
- Honey, for drizzling
- Sea salt

Instructions:

Heat your grill to medium-high. Then, grease peaches with oil and grill for around 4 to 5 minutes until soft. Flipping the skin-side down and grill it more 4 to 6 minutes until soft. Serve your peaches with ice cream, spray honey, and a sprinkling of sea salt.

2.4 Grilled Pineapple

Prep time: 10 mins

Cooking time: 15 mins

Servings: 4

Ingredients:

- One ripe, quartered, peeled, and cored pineapple
- Two tablespoons of packed brown sugar
- Juice of 1 lime

Instructions:

Preheat your grill or grill pan to high heat. Roll together lime juice, pineapple, and brown sugar in a bowl. Then, Place on the grill and cook for 10 to 15 minutes until you can easily put a stick into the center of a piece. Your grilled pineapple is ready to serve.

2.5 Grilled Pineapple Sundaes

Prep time: 10 mins

Cooking time: 10 mins

Servings: 4

Ingredients:

- Four slices of pineapple

- Four scoops of vanilla ice cream

- Dulce de leche, for drizzling

- Two tablespoons of sweetened shredded coconut, toasted

Instructions:

Heat your grill to high heat and grill for around 1 minute until charred. Coat each pineapple slice with the vanilla ice cream and spray with the caramel or dulce de leche. Top with the shredded coconut, and serve your grilled pineapple immediately.

2.6 Grilled Pizza Bread

Prep time: 10 mins

Cooking time: 15 mins

Servings: 6

Ingredients:

- 1/3 cups pepperoni

- One large halved loaf

- 1/4 cups black olives

- 3 cups of shredded mozzarella

- Half red onions, cut into half

- 1 chopped Bell Pepper, green

- 1/2 red onions, cut into thin half-moons

- 1 15ounce jar of pizza sauce

- Red pepper flakes in a pinch amount, grounded

Instructions:

Remove the middle parts from bread halves in order to create shape of deep boats. Pour the pizza sauce on every half, then coat with pepperoni, mozzarella, red pepper flakes, red onion, black

olives, and green bell pepper. Then, wrap the bread with foil of aluminium then put it over a grill fire and let it cook for 10 to 15 minutes until your cheese melts and your crust gets toasted. Let it cool for around 12 mins before slicing. Now, serve your food.

2.7 Reese's Cones

Prep time: 10 mins

Cooking time: 10 mins

Servings: 6

Ingredients:

- Six waffle cones

- peanut butter

- Reese's miniature cups

- Mini marshmallows

- Reese's pieces

Instructions:

Stuff your cones with some marshmallows, Reese's Pieces, peanut butter and Reese's cups. Then, wrap your cones using foil then put them on the grill fire for 5 minutes until your candies get melted. Remove from flame and then let it cool to handle the cones. Cones are ready to serve.

2.8 Campfire Cobbler

Prep time: 15 mins

Cooking time: 1 hour and 15 mins

Servings: 6

Ingredients:

- 1 cup of blueberries
- Six chopped peaches
- 1/4 cup plus two tablespoons sugar, divided
- 1 cup of chopped strawberries
- Two tablespoons of cornstarch
- pinch of kosher salt
- Two tablespoons of ground cinnamon
- 2 cups of raspberries
- 2 1/3 cup of Bisquick Mix
- 1/2 cup of milk

Instructions:

Combine fruits, cinnamon, 1/4 cup of sugar, salt, and cornstarch in a large plastic bag. Seal the bag tightly and shake until fruit is evenly coated. In the other reseal able plastic bag, combine milk and Bisquick. Then, Seal and mix, kneading by using hands, until completely combined. Grease a large cast-iron skillet with butter. Add the fruit mixture and roll with Bisquick topping. Spray 2 tablespoons of the remaining sugar. Now, cover with foil and cook over a campfire for 50 minutes until your biscuits are no longer doughy and fruit is warm; let it cool for 20 minutes, then serve your delicious food.

2.9 Panzanella Peach with Burrata

Prep time: 10 mins

Cooking time: 10 mins

Servings: 4

Ingredients:

- 1/2 loaf of ciabatta and cut in 1 1/2 cubes

- One 8-ounce of ball burrata

- 1/2 thinly sliced red onion

- 1/2 cup of white balsamic vinegar

- kosher salt

- Freshly grounded black pepper

- 1/2 cup of olive oil extra-virgin divided

- Eight small (or four large) ripe peaches

- 1/2 cup of torn fresh basil leaves, plus more for serving

Instructions:

Preheat your grill to 425° and combine balsamic vinegar and red onion in a small bowl. On a baking sheet, mix the bread cubes in 1 tablespoon of olive oil and season with the salt. Bake for 5 minutes until crisp, then let it cool.

Gently roll peaches with one tablespoon of olive oil and season with pepper and salt. Then, heat your grill or grill pan over medium-high heat. Grill peaches for 2-3 minutes until slightly charred, then flip and grill for 2 minutes more. Now, transfer to a baking sheet to let it cool.

Pour ¼ cup of balsamic vinegar from the marinated onions into a bowl and stir in 6 tablespoons of olive oil, then season them with salt and pepper. Strain onions and discard the remaining vinegar, then add bread cubes, onions, and basil peaches to a large bowl. Gently toss with the vinaigrette. Divide Panzanella onto the four plates and coat each with burrata. Garnish with basil and a spray of olive oil. Serve your food immediately.

2.10 Grilled Fruit Skewers

Prep time: 10 mins

Cooking time: 5 mins

Servings: 8

Ingredients:

- kosher salt
- Six sliced peaches
- One pineapple and cut into large cubes
- 1 pint of sliced Strawberries,
- Eight skewers, soaked in water for 20 minutes
- Olive oil Extra-virgin, for drizzling
- Honey, for the drizzling

Instructions:

Preheat your grill to medium-high and skewer strawberries, peaches, and pineapple. Then, spray with olive oil and season with salt. Grill for around 10 minutes, flipping occasionally until the fruit is tender and slightly charred. Now, spray honey and serve your food.

2.11 Grilled Roasted Pepper and Portobello Sandwich with Pistachio Style Pesto

Prep time: 5 mins

Cooking time: 15 mins

Servings: 1

Ingredients:

- One portobello mushroom
- Olive oil
- Balsamic vinegar
- One red roasted pepper

- One tablespoon of pistachio pesto

- One handful spinach

- Two bread slices

Instructions:

Brush your mushroom with some balsamic vinegar, then brush the grill with some oil and then grill the portobello mushroom until it is tender for about three to six minutes per side. Assemble the sandwich.

2.12 Grilled Chicken Curry Salad with Vinaigrette Herb

Prep time: Half-hour

Cooking time: 15 mins

Servings: 4

Ingredients:

- One tablespoon of Olive oil

- Two skinless and boneless chicken breasts

- Two tablespoons of Curry powder

- One teaspoon of black pepper

- Two teaspoons of salt

- 4 cups of Spring greens

- Pickled onions

- One sliced Mango

- Four ounces of Chevre goat cheese

- 1/4 cup of Torn mint leaves

- 1/4 cup of Cilantro leaves

- One small chopped shallot

- 3/4 cup of Olive oil

- 1/4 teaspoon of black pepper

- One teaspoon of Dijon mustard

- 1/4 cup of Rice vinegar

- One teaspoon of Honey

- 1/4 cup of packed cilantro

- Half teaspoon of salt

- One smashed clove of Garlic

- 1/4 cup of mint Torn leaves

Instructions:

Preheat your grill to low-medium. Combine salt, olive oil, curry powder and pepper in a bowl and rub chicken breasts with the mixture of curry powder and set it on the grill. Then cook until the internal temperature of the chicken shows 165°F on an instant thermometer. Try turning often to evade drying out, and once it is finished, let it rest for about some minutes before cutting it into slices that are thick. In a blender, mix all dressing of salad ingredients and then blend until it is smooth and will store it up to a week in your refrigerator in a sealed container. On four plates, cut the prepared chicken, spring greens and other ingredients and then drizzle with a proper amount of dressing. Serve immediately.

2.13 Stone Grilled Fruit with Granola and Yogurt

Prep time: 10 mins

Cooking time: 10 mins

Servings: 6

Ingredients:

- Three halved peaches

- One tablespoon of canola oil

- Three halved plums

- One cup of Siggi's plain yogurt

- One tablespoon of honey

- One teaspoon of the paste of vanilla bean

- Homemade Granola flavored as Vanilla Almond

Instructions:

Preheat the grill to moderate temperature (300 degrees -350 degrees F). Brush the flesh part of the fruit halves with canola oil. Combine yogurt, honey and vanilla paste in a small bowl. Combine all ingredients in a mixing bowl and place aside. Place the stone fruit on the grill with the flesh part down. Grill for around 4-5 minutes, or until char marks emerge. Take it off the grill. Serve stone fruit which is grilled with a spoonful of vanilla yogurt (about a tbsp.) mixture and homemade almond granola on top. Drizzle using honey as a finishing touch if desired.

2.14 Bbq Style Fruit Salad

Prep time: 20 mins

Cooking time: 8 mins

Servings: 4

Ingredients:

- Two tablespoons of honey

- Half teaspoon of cinnamon

- Two tablespoons of coconut oil

- One teaspoon maple or honey syrup

- One teaspoon of vanilla

- Four rounds of pineapple that are cut into thirds

- Two cut and pitted plums into quarters

- Two cut and pitted nectarines into eighths

- Three pitted apricots and halved

- Ten halved strawberries

- 1/2 cup of blueberries

- Two tablespoons of chopped fresh mint

Instructions:

Preheat the grill to a high temperature. Combine the cinnamon, coconut oil, vanilla extract and honey, in a frying pan over moderate heat and whisk to melt the coconut oil and cook until it starts to mildly bubble. Take the pan off the flame and apply the cinnamon. Pour the honey mixture and coconut oil over the pineapple slices, nectarines, apricots and plums in a big mixing bowl. Shake the fruit using the hands to uniformly cover it. Place the apricots, plums, pineapple and nectarines on the grill and grill for around 3 minutes on each side or until grill lines emerge. Toss the blueberries plus strawberries in leftover honey liquid and coconut at the base of the bowl when the fruit is grilling. To eat, toss the cooked fruit with the blueberries and strawberries on a platter or in a bowl, cover with minced mint, and spoon a cup of lemon cream or coconut cream on top.

2.15 Grilled Apricots

Prep time: 10 mins

Cooking time: 15 mins

Servings: 4

Ingredients:

- Two peaches or apricots pitted and halved

- 4 Tablespoons of chopped toasted walnuts

- Two cups of plain Greek yogurt

- 4 Tablespoons of maple syrup

Instructions:

Preheat a grill, a stovetop pan, or a broiler to high temperature. Cook for around 5 minutes, or until the fruit is beautifully browned on the outside. The fruit must be softened but still retain the shape. Top every fruit half using a half cup of yogurt, 1 tbsp. walnuts, and 1 tbsp. maple syrup.

2.16 Barbecued Grilled Autumn Style Fruit with Thyme and Honey sabayon

Prep time: 15 minutes

Cooking time: 10 minutes

Servings: 2-3

Ingredients:

- One apple

- Quince, which is medium-sized

- 1 pear

- Half lemon

- Two plums

- Honey

- Two tablespoons of water

- Four yolks of egg

- Five thyme sprigs

- Quarter bunch of thyme stalks reserved and leaves picked

- Marsala wine 50ml

Instructions:

Set the barbecue for direct cooking by lighting it. Secure the quince in foil and set aside. Once the coals become ashen-grey, gently nestle the packet into them using long-handled tongs, ensuring it's entirely coated in coals plus ash. Shut the lid and simmer for around 40 minutes or until the product is done. To save the apple plus pear from browning, quarter them, core them, and pour some drops of lemon juice on them, spreading it over the diced surfaces. Place the pear, apple, and plums on a wide plate and chill for around 20 minutes to partially dry them out. Prepare the thyme syrup in the meantime. In a shallow saucepan, combine the water, honey and thyme. Boil mixture over medium temperature on the stovetop then places aside to incorporate for around 5 minutes. In a big heatproof dish, whisk together the Marsala, egg yolks, thyme leaves and honey and place over a pan containing simmering water for the sabayon. Regularly whisk the sabayon solution (hand-held automatic beaters work well) until it crystallizes and expands in volume; it's crucial to keep stirring so the solution doesn't 'cook' on the bottom of the bowl scattering the egg yolks. The sabayon must be pale, light and airy when done. Keep warm and reserve. Brush the thyme syrup over the pear, plums and apple. Position the stored thyme stalks on the grill to heat, then position the fruit and shut the lid. Cook for around 5 minutes, or until mildly charred, then flip and spray using thyme syrup again. Grill the plums for around three extra minutes, and the apple plus pear for around five extra minutes, or until tender and charred. In the meantime, verify that the quince is done through and tender – a knife can glide in easily – then set aside for about five minutes to cool before separating the foil. Dice quince into quarters with a tiny knife or with a spoon and remove the core, then drizzle the thyme syrup over quince quarters. If the fruit's surface seems to be too burnt, just strip it off. Serve using the sabayon and some thyme syrup leftover.

2.17 A La Mode Barbecued Apples

Prep time: 5 minutes

Cooking time: 25 minutes

Servings: 4

Ingredients:

- Two tablespoons of butter (or for vegan use coconut oil)
- Two firm apples which are tart-sweet (like Granny Jonathon, Smith, Honey Crisp, Fuji, gala, etc.)
- A quarter teaspoon of nutmeg
- Two tablespoons of brown sugar
- One teaspoon of cinnamon
- Two tablespoons of white sugar
- A quarter teaspoon of ginger
- For serving: whipped cream or vanilla ice cream (or whipped cream of vegan)

Instructions:

Heat the grill to moderate temperature (375 degrees to 450 degrees). Slice the apples into quarter-inch strips. Put the apples on a big sheet of aluminum foil and wrap it around them. Top with thinly sliced butter, cinnamon, sugar, ginger, plus nutmeg. Toss them together with your fingertips. Place another layer of foil on top and make holes in it using a fork to secure it. Grill for around 20 to 25 minutes over the indirect fire or until apples is tender. Serve with ice cream on top (either direct on the foil or transfer to bowls).

2.18 Grilled and Barbecued Bananas

Prep time: 10 minutes

Cooking time: 10 minutes

Servings: 4

Ingredients:

- A quarter cup of pure syrup of maple
- Four bananas which are ripe but firm
- 1/4 teaspoon of ground ginger
- One tablespoon of neutral oil
- 1/4 teaspoon of ground nutmeg
- One teaspoon of ground cinnamon
- For serving: ice cream vanilla (vegan as essential), toasted chopped pecans or pecans which are glazed

Instructions:

Heat the grill to moderate temperature (375 degrees to 450 degrees F). Stir together the oil, maple syrup, cinnamon, ginger and nutmeg in a medium bowl. Remove the banana peels stem, thus keeping the peel on. The banana can then be cut in half long ways. Brush the sliced side of the bananas using half of the maple mixture. Grill for around 3 to 4 minutes, placing diced side down until you see grill marks. Cook for another 4 or 5 minutes, or until tender. To eat, use a spoon to scoop the bananas out of their peels. Drizzle using maple mixture after stirring it. Serve using ice cream and sliced pecans.

Chapter 03: Poultry food

This chapter will help you to learn and experiment with the different basic varieties of recipes that can be made by using poultry regarding grilling. It definitely consists of an infinite number of options to try according to your taste buds. All the recipes are given in detail with the particular ingredients and instructions to guide you in making your chicken more delicious using grilling techniques.

3.1 Grilled Sticky Chicken

Prep time: 10 mins

Cooking time: 2 hours and 25 mins

Servings: 4

Ingredients:

- 1/2 cup low-sodium soy sauce

- Three tablespoon honey

- 1/2 cup balsamic vinegar

- Two cloves of garlic that are minced

- Two tablespoons of sesame seeds

- Two and a half chicken drumsticks

- Two thinly sliced green onions

- Vegetable oil

Instructions:

Take a bowl, stir together balsamic vinegar, soy sauce, green onions, honey and garlic. Set aside one-fourth cup of marinade, then add chicken to a reseal able bag made of plastic and then pour in leftover marinade. Let them marinate in the fridge for 2 hours. When ready to grill, heat the grill to high. Oil the surface and grill chicken, turning every 3- 4 minutes and 30 minutes total until it cooked and charred through. Garnish it with the seeds before serving. Enjoy your food.

3.2 Grilled Chicken Wings

Prep time: 10 mins

Cooking time: 25 mins

Servings: 4

Ingredients:

For making wings:

- Two teaspoons of kosher salt
- Zest of lime
- One teaspoon of smoked paprika
- Onion powder, one teaspoon
- One teaspoon of garlic powder
- One teaspoon of thyme, dried
- 2 pound of chicken wings
- A quarter teaspoon of cayenne
- Vegetable oil

For making sauce:

- Juice of half lime
- Half cup of mayonnaise
- One teaspoon of hot sauce
- One tablespoon of Dijon mustard
- Two teaspoons of chives, chopped
- Horseradish, two teaspoons

Instructions:

Stir together paprika, salt, garlic powder, lemon zest, onion powder, cayenne and thyme in a bowl. Take wings of chicken and add some spices. Then, heat the grill or grill plate to medium heat and grease the grates using vegetable oil. Now, it is time to add wings and cook until the skin looks crisp and the meat is cooked fully for 15 to 20 minutes. Now prepare your sauce stir together mayo, mustard, lemon juice, chives, horseradish, and hot sauce. Serve your chicken wings hot with the dipping sauce.

3.3 California Grilled Chicken

Prep time: 20 mins

Cooking time: 30 mins

Servings: 4

Ingredients:

- One teaspoon of garlic powder
- A three-fourth cup of balsamic vinegar
- Two tablespoons of honey
- Two teaspoons of seasoning, Italian
- Two tablespoons of extra-virgin olive oil
- Kosher salt
- Balsamic glaze
- Four boneless breasts of chicken
- Black pepper, grounded freshly
- Mozzarella, four slices
- Tomato, four slices
- Four slices of avocado
- Two tablespoons of sliced basil

Instructions:

Stir together garlic powder, balsamic vinegar, oil, honey, and Italian seasoning and season them with pepper and salt now, put it over chicken and marinate for 20 minutes. When it is ready to grill, heat the grill to medium-high. Oil surface and grill chicken until cooked for 8 minutes per side. Coat chicken with avocado, mozzarella, and tomato and then cover grill to melt for 2 minutes. Garnish with basil and sprinkle with balsamic glaze.

3.4 Grilled Chicken Breast

Prep time: 15 mins

Cooking time: 30 mins

Servings: 4

Ingredients:

- One-fourth cup of balsamic vinegar

- Two tablespoons of brown sugar

- Three cloves of minced garlic

- Kosher salt

- One tablespoon of dried thyme

- One tablespoon of dried rosemary

- Chopped parsley for garnishing

- Four chicken breasts

- Three tablespoons of olive oil extra-virgin

- Black pepper freshly ground

Instructions:

Stir together olive oil, balsamic vinegar, brown sugar, and dried herbs garlic in a bowl and season them with salt and pepper. Reserve one-fourth cup and then add chicken to the bowl and toss them to mix. Let marinate for 20 minutes and up to overnight. Now, preheat your grill to medium-high. Add chicken and grill until it is cooked for 6 minutes per side. Garnish with the parsley before serving to your guest.

3.5 Spiral Grilled Hot Dogs

Prep time: 20 mins

Cooking time: 10 mins

Servings: 4

Ingredients:

- Four buns

- One wooden skewer

- Four hot dogs

- Assorted toppings for serving

Instructions:

Heat your grill. Slide a long wooden skewer through the whole of your hot dog. Put your hot dog on the cutting board and cut it into pieces by using the knife. Flip the hot dog and continue cutting until you reach the end. Now, carefully remove the skewer from the hot dog. Repeat the process with the remaining dogs and grill for around 8 minutes. Serve in the buns immediately with your favorite toppings.

3.6 Jerk Chicken

Prep time: 10 mins

Cooking time: 150 mins

Servings: 4

Ingredients:

- One roughly chopped jalapeño

- ½ tablespoon of ground cinnamon

- One bunch of green onions, plus more thinly sliced for garnish

- Two garlic cloves

- Two tablespoons of olive oil extra-virgin

- One tablespoon of packed brown sugar

- Juice of 1 lime

- Kosher salt

- 1 ½ tablespoon of ground allspice

- Vegetable oil for the grill

- One tablespoon of dried thyme

- Eight pieces of bone-in chicken drumsticks and thighs

Instructions:

Combine garlic, green onions, brown sugar, jalapeno, lime juice, oil, allspice, cinnamon, one teaspoon salt, thyme, and two tablespoons water in a blender and blend them until smooth. Put the chicken in a shallow dish and season with the salt. Now, pour the remaining marinade over chicken and roll to coat. Let it marinate in the fridge, at least for 2 hours or up to overnight.

When ready to grill, heat your grill to medium-high heat and oil the surface. Grill chicken for around 10 minutes turning each occasionally, until the chicken is charred. Now, move your chicken to a cooler part of the grill and brush with the rest of the marinade. Then, cover your grill until the chicken is cooked.

3.7 Popper Jalapeño Dogs

Prep time: 10 mins

Cooking time: 30 mins

Servings: 4

Ingredients:

- Four hot dog buns

- 12 jalapeños extra large

- Four thin halved lengthwise hot dogs

- 8 American cheese slices

- Mustard

Instructions:

Heat the grill at high temperature. Cut the bottoms where it's narrowing and the tops. Remove ribs & seeds. Put rectangular cheese pieces in the center of hot dogs. Then put these hot dogs in the peppers. Grill till the cheese melts but not so much. Serve with the buns used with hot dog and enjoy.

3.8 Grilled Bruschetta Chicken

Prep time: 20 minutes

Cooking time: 1 hour and 10 mins

Servings: 4

Ingredients:

- Four tablespoons of olive oil extra-virgin
- Juice of 1 lemon, divided
- Kosher salt
- Black pepper Freshly ground
- One tablespoon of dried oregano or Italian seasoning
- Four boneless chicken breasts skinless antibiotic-free pounded to even thickness
- Three chopped tomatoes
- Two cloves of garlic, chopped
- One tablespoon of freshly chopped basil
- Four slices of mozzarella
- Freshly grated Parmesan for the serving

Instructions:

Combine oil, one teaspoon of salt, half the lemon juice, and Italian seasoning (or oregano), and 1 /4 teaspoon pepper and stir to combine in a bowl. Transfer it to a large reseal able bag with the chicken, seal and refrigerate them for 30 minutes. Heat your grill over medium-high, then add chicken, and discard the excessive marinate. Grill the chicken until charred and cooked for around 5 to 7 minutes to a temperature of 165 degrees per side. Meanwhile, combine the ingredients like garlic, tomatoes, basil, and remaining lemon juice, then season with salt and pepper. While the chicken is still on the grill, coat each breast with one slice of the mozzarella and cover it until cheese is melted; coat chicken with the tomato mixture. Now, garnish with the Parmesan and serve this to your guest.

3.9 Salsa Grilled Verde Chicken

Prep time: 20 mins

Cooking time: Half-hour

Servings: 4

Ingredients:

- One jar of salsa verde
- 1/2 lime Juiced
- Two garlic cloves, minced
- ½ tablespoon of powdered cumin
- 1 lb. skinless boneless chicken breasts
- Four slices of Monterey jack
- ½ tablespoon of chili powder
- One thinly sliced jalapeño
- Two tablespoons of olive oil extra-virgin
- ½ finely chopped red onion
- Two tablespoons cilantro freshly chopped
- Lime wedges

Instructions:

In a container, mix half cup salsa, olive oil, garlic, lime juice cumin and chili powder. Save half cup salsa for chicken and half to serve it with. Coat the chicken with it and let it sit for twenty minutes. Heat the grill to med-hi, then place chicken over it and let it cook for about six minutes. Place cheese pieces over each chicken breast and let it grill till the cheese melts for about four minutes.

3.10 Peppers and Sausage Foil Pack

Prep time: 10 mins

Cooking time: 20 mins

Servings: 4

Ingredients:

- Four thinly sliced bell peppers
- kosher salt
- Two large thinly sliced onions
- 8 Italian sausage links
- Freshly ground black pepper
- 1/4 cup of olive oil extra-virgin
- Chopped fresh parsley for garnish

Instructions:

Heat your grill to high and cut four sheets of foil about 12" long. Grill sausages for 3 minutes per side until charred, then divide among the foil. Roll sausages with peppers and onions and sprinkle with one tablespoon of olive oil, then season with pepper and salt. Fold foil packets crosswise over the sausage and peppers mixture to completely cover your food. Roll-top and bottom edges to seal the ends. Grill for 13 to 15 minutes until peppers and onions are tender and sausage is cooked. Garnish with parsley and serve the food to your guests.

3.11 Tomatoes Chicken and Corn Foil Packs

Prep time: 10 mins

Cooking time: 20 mins

Servings: 4

Ingredients:

- Two ears of corn, kernels stripped
- Kosher salt
- Four boneless skinless chicken breasts

- 2 cups of halved grape tomatoes

- 1/4 cup of olive oil extra-virgin

- Two tablespoons of butter

- Two garlic cloves thinly sliced

- Black pepper freshly ground

Instructions:

Heat your grill to high and cut about 12" long four sheets of foil. Roll every piece of your foil with chicken breast, garlic, corn, and tomatoes. Spray each with the oil and roll with a pat of butter. Then, Season it with pepper and salt. Now, fold the packets of foil crosswise over the chicken and roll top and bottom edges to seal it. Grill for 15 to 20 minutes until the chicken is fully cooked through and vegetables are tender. Serve topped with basil. Enjoy your food.

3.12 Teriyaki Chicken with Pineapple Yakitori

Prep time: 15 mins

Cooking time: 30 mins

Servings: 5

Ingredients:

- Six skinless, boneless chicken thighs and cut into bite-sized pieces

- kosher salt

- Black pepper freshly ground

- 1/2 pineapple and cut into one piece

- Two cloves of minced garlic

- Steamed white rice for the serving

- Three green onions and cut into one piece

- Toasted sesame seeds for the garnishing

- Two tablespoons of cornstarch

- 1/4 cup of low-sodium soy sauce

- 1/4 cup of water

- Four tablespoons of honey

- Two tablespoons of pineapple juice

- Two tablespoons of rice wine vinegar

Instructions:

Preheat your grill to 375 degrees. Spear, chicken, pineapple, and green onion pieces onto each skewer, turning off between the ingredients until each of your skewers are filled. Season with salt and pepper. For the sauce, add all of your ingredients to a saucepan and stir together. Put mixture over the medium heat and cook for about 10 minutes until your mixture has thickened enough to coat the back of a spoon.

Grill each skewer for 5 to 6 minutes until the chicken has cooked through. Coat skewers with teriyaki sauce on both sides and grill for 30 seconds more. Now, put skewers over the steamed rice and roll with sesame seeds. Serve this with more sauce on the side, if you desired. Enjoy your food.

3.13 Grilled Hot Dogs

Prep time: 10 mins

Cooking time: 10 mins

Servings: 6

Ingredients:

- Barbecue sauce

- Six pieces of romaine lettuce

- Six hot dogs which we used for chicken, regular, and veggie

- Dill pickles

- White onion, finely chopped

Instructions:

Grill the type of hot dogs according to the directions given on the package. Spread romaine leaves and position the grilled hot dogs on them. Top with toppings of your preference.

3.14 Hawaiian Chicken Skewers

Prep time: 25 mins

Cooking time: 10 mins

Servings: 4

Ingredients:

- 1/3 cup of soy sauce
- One tablespoon of rice wine vinegar
- 1/2 cup of barbecue sauce
- Two tablespoons of sesame oil
- one tablespoon of minced ginger
- one tablespoon of honey
- two minced cloves of garlic
- kosher salt
- two chicken breasts and cut into 1" pieces
- two cups of cubed pineapple
- one tablespoon of crushed red pepper flakes
- two green diced bell peppers
- one red diced onion
- two tablespoons of cilantro
- White rice, for serving

Instructions:

Preheat the grill pan or grill to moderate heat. Whisk together soy sauce, barbecue sauce, vinegar, garlic, oil, ginger, plus honey in a big mixing bowl until well mixed. Season using pepper and salt according to taste. Add chicken, peppers, red onion and pineapple on skewers. Position on a baking tray and sprinkle half of the marinade over it. Brush skewers with the rest of the marinade and positions them on preheated grill. Cook for five minutes before flipping and coating the other surface using the marinade. Grill until the chicken is thoroughly cooked for five more minutes. Eat with rice and add cilantro on top.

3.15 Chicken BBQ with Sweet Chili Peach Glaze

Prep time: 10 mins

Cooking time: 30 mins

Servings: 4

Ingredients:

- 1/2 cup of sweet chili sauce
- Juice and zest of 1 lime
- Five peaches, sliced in half and pitted, divided
- Eight green onions
- Two red onions, sliced into 3/4" rings
- 2 pound of bone-in skin-on chicken thighs
- Olive oil type extra-virgin for drizzling
- Bamboo skewers, soaked in water
- kosher salt
- Freshly ground black pepper

Instructions:

In a food processor, add sweet chili sauce, one peach (roughly cut), zest and lime juice; process and blend until soft; then move to a small cup. Place the rest of the peaches, sliced side up, on a rimmed pan with green onions. Place onions on a sheet pan after skewering them through the center. Toss with a light drizzle of olive oil until evenly colored. Season using pepper and salt. Preheat the grill to medium-high temperature. Meanwhile, thoroughly clean the chicken and allow it to dry. Place the chicken on a different rimmed pan and drizzle using olive oil; season using pepper and salt.

Place the chicken on the grill and cover. Cook for around 10 minutes. Add peaches, onions and green onions after flipping the chicken. Cover and cook for around 5 minutes before flipping the peaches & vegetables. Rub glaze on chicken as it hits a core temperature of 150 degrees to 155 degrees F. Cook, for another 25 minutes or until the chicken is glazed and golden brown on all sides and the core temperature reaches 165 degrees. Grilling time is around 10 minutes, and peaches, as well as vegetables, should have black grill marks and be mildly charred. Transfer to a big platter and drizzle with the remaining glaze before serving.

3.16 Grilled Balsamic Chicken with Zucchini

Prep time: 10 mins

Cooking time: 25 mins

Servings: 5

Ingredients:

- 1/2 cup of balsamic vinegar
- One tablespoon of orange zest
- 1/2 cup of honey
- One tablespoon of chopped fresh oregano
- Two medium yellow zucchini about 1 pound
- Two medium green zucchini about 1 pound
- Sea salt, such as Maldon
- 1 1/2 pound of Tyson Boneless Skinless Chicken Breasts, pounded to 1/2" thickness
- Olive oil
- kosher salt
- Freshly ground black pepper

Instructions:

Combine honey plus balsamic vinegar in a shallow saucepan over moderate heat. Boil the mixture, and then simmer for around 10 minutes, or until moderately thickened. Remove from heat and stir in the orange zest plus oregano. 1/4 cup is set aside for serving. Trim each end of every zucchini in the meantime. By sliding the blade against the surface of each zucchini with a vegetable peeler or a mandolin, make long straight noodles. Put aside after seasoning with salt.

Preheat the grill to moderate temperatures. Season Skinless and boneless Chicken Breasts with pepper and salt after drizzling with olive oil. Cook the chicken for around 4 minutes on either side of the barbecue. Cook until the chicken is finely crispy all over and the internal temperature hits 170 degrees, around 2 to 3 minutes. Plastic wrap loosely and transfer to a clean tray. Get a stockpot of water (8-quart) to a boil, seasoning liberally with salt. Cook zucchini for around 3 minutes, or until al dente, then drain. With a spoon of honey-balsamic glaze and a pinch of sea salt, cut chicken against the grain and eat with zucchini noodles.

3.17 Greek Grilled Chicken Kebabs

Prep time: 20 mins

Cooking time: 10 mins

Servings: 4

Ingredients:

- Three tablespoons red wine vinegar
- One tablespoon of dried oregano
- kosher salt
- 1 cup of olive oil, divided
- Freshly ground black pepper
- 1/4 cup of torn fresh dill
- Two large zucchini, cut into half-moons
- 1 cup of chopped red onion (in 1" pieces)
- 1 pound of boneless skinless chicken breasts, cut into cubes
- Four pitas
- 1/2 cup of crumbled feta

Instructions:

Preheat the grill to moderate temperature. To make the marinade, follow these steps: Mix together vinegar, 3/4 cup of olive oil, and oregano in a big bowl, season using pepper and salt. Half of the mixture is set aside for later use. Toss the chicken with the marinade until it is well mixed. Add Chicken on skewers with zucchini & red onion. Season skewers using pepper and salt and drizzle with the leftover 1/4 cup of olive oil. Grill for around 5 minutes on each side on medium heat until crispy and cooked through. Place on a serving platter and serve. Grill for around 30 seconds. Serve the skewers in pitas with feta, dill, and the marinade that was reserved.

3.18 Chicago Grilled Dogs

Prep time: 5 mins

Cooking time: 10 mins

Servings: 4

Ingredients:

- Bread and sliced butter pickles
- 1 cup of sliced cherry tomatoes
- Eight hot dogs
- Eight potato buns of hot dog
- sweet pickle relish
- 1 cup of shredded lettuce
- 1/4 cup of Chopped white onion
- Yellow mustard, for the serving

Instructions:

Preheat your grill or grill pan over medium-high heat and cook your hot dogs for 2 minutes on each side. Then, assemble the hot dogs and Line bun with the pickle slices, then add hot dog and coat with onions, tomatoes, relish and lettuce. Spray with mustard and serve your food.

3.19 Bbq Chicken with Lime Chili Corn

Prep time: 5 mins

Cooking time: 45 mins

Servings: 4

Ingredients:

- Two skin-on, bone-in chicken breasts
- Two skin-on, bone-in chicken thighs and legs
- kosher salt
- black pepper
- 2 cups of barbecue sauce
- 1/2 cup of Original Country Crock
- One tablespoon of lime zest grated
- One tablespoon of lime juice
- One tablespoon of chili powder
- ½ tsp of cumin
- 4 corn ears and remove husks
- Lime wedges

Instructions:

Preheat grill at high. Season the meat with pepper and salt and grill for about 15 minutes over lightly greased grate, flipping once. Add 1 cup bbq sauce and let it cook for next fifteen minutes. Add one more cup of bbq sauce and grill for another fifteen minutes. In the meantime mix country crock, lime juice, zest, cumin and chili powder. Add pepper and salt. 15 minutes prior to chicken is cooked, rub the corn with half of the lime paste. Grill till soft. Once done serve with more lime paste and enjoy.

3.20 Italian Chicken Skewers

Prep time: 15 mins

Cooking time: 10 mins

Servings: 8

Ingredients:

- Black pepper Freshly ground

- 1 pound of boneless skinless chicken breasts and cut into large cubes

- One baguette of French bread and cut into cubes

- kosher salt

- Two tablespoons of tomato paste

- Three minced garlic cloves

- One tablespoon of chopped fresh Italian parsley, plus more leaves for garnish

- 1/4 cup of olive oil extra-virgin, plus more for drizzling

- Eight skewers, soaked in water for 20 minutes

Instructions:

Season chicken with pepper and salt. Combine olive oil, garlic cloves, tomato paste and chopped parsley in a large bowl to make the marinade. Add chicken and roll to fully coat and refrigerate for 30 minutes. Then, preheat your grill to medium-high. Skewer chicken and bread. Spray with olive oil and season with the salt and pepper. Now, grill for around 10 minutes, occasionally flipping until the chicken is cooked through and the bread is slightly charred. Garnish with parsley and serve.

3.21 Chicken Bbq Souvlaki

Prep time: 5 minutes

Cooking time: 10 minutes

Servings: 4

Ingredients:

- One pound skinless and boneless chicken thighs or breasts
- Two chopped cloves of garlic
- One lemon, zest and juice
- One tablespoon of yogurt
- A quarter cup of olive oil
- One teaspoon of oregano
- A quarter teaspoon of salt
- A quarter teaspoon of pepper

Instructions:

Refrigerate the chicken for around 30 minutes up to overnight after marinating it in the rest of the ingredients. Place chicken on the grill and cook until tender, around 4 minutes on each side, over moderate flame.

3.22 Dakkochi

Prep time: 60 mins

Cooking time: 15 mins

Servings: 4

Ingredients:

- One pound of chicken breast
- Three cloves of grated garlic
- One inch of grated ginger
- Half small grated onion

- Half Asian grated pear

- A quarter cup of soy sauce

- Half tablespoon of sesame oil

- Half tablespoon of brown sugar

- One green chopped onions

- 1/4 teaspoon of pepper

Instructions:

In a freezer bag, combine all of the ingredients and marinate for a minimum of an hour. Prepare the chicken by skewering it on wet skewers and set it aside. Take solids out of the marinade and cook it for around 5-10 minutes, or before it builds up and turns saucy. Grill the chicken for around 5 minutes a side on the grill, dripping it using the marinade as you go.

3.23 Grilled Moroccan Chicken Kabobs

Prep time: 20 mins

Cooking time: 10 mins

Servings: 4

Ingredients:

- 1 pound skinless and boneless chicken, which is cut into small pieces

- Two tablespoons of lemon juice

- Two tablespoons of olive oil

- One teaspoon of paprika

- Half teaspoon of the ground and toasted cumin

- 1/8 teaspoon of cinnamon

- 1/8 teaspoon of ginger

- A quarter teaspoon of turmeric

- A quarter teaspoon of cayenne

- A quarter teaspoon of salt

- A quarter teaspoon of pepper

- Two chopped cloves of garlic

Instructions:

Mix chicken with the rest of the ingredients and place in the fridge for around 20 minutes or upto overnight to let it marinate in the mixture. Add chicken to skewers and grill until tender, around 4-5 minutes on each side, over moderate temperature.

3.24 Tandoori Bbq Chicken

Prep time: 2 hours

Cooking time: 30 mins

Servings: 4

Ingredients:

- Half juice of the lemon

- Half cup of plain yogurt

- Half small grated onion

- One tablespoon of grated ginger

- One tablespoon of grated garlic

- Half teaspoon of cayenne pepper

- One tablespoon of garam masala

- One teaspoon of the ground and toasted cumin

- 1 pound of boneless skinless and chicken (1 inch pieces)

- One tablespoon of paprika

- One teaspoon of the ground and toasted coriander

Salt to taste

Instructions:

Mix everything, except the chicken, in a bowl. Put the chicken with the mixture in a reseal able bag and marinate by placing it in the fridge for at least an hour up to a maximum of 24 hours. Take the chicken out of the refrigerator and set it aside to fall to room temperature. Skewer the chicken after extracting it from the bag. Grill, the chicken for around 5 minutes on each side on the grill.

3.25 Grilled Japanese Chicken Skewers

Prep time: 20 mins

Cooking time: 10 mins

Servings: 4

Ingredients:

- Three tablespoons of soy sauce

- Three tablespoons of mirin

- Two tablespoons of sake

- One tablespoon of sugar

- 1 pound of chicken thigh or breast, bite-sized pieces

Instructions:

Bring the mirin, soy sauce, sugar and sake to a boil, then lower the heat and cook until the mixture thickens slightly around 5 minutes. Mix chicken with half sauce mixture and marinate by placing in the fridge for around 20 minutes or up to a maximum of 24 hours. Using skewers, thread the chicken. Grill until tender, around 2-4 minutes on each side over moderate temperature, dripping with the remaining sauce before serving.

3.26 Grilled Lime Taco Style Chicken

Prep time: 5 mins

Cooking time: 10 mins

Servings: 4

Ingredients:

- Two tablespoons of taco seasoning

- A quarter cup of lime juice

- 1 pound of skinless and boneless chicken breasts

Instructions:

Combine the taco seasoning plus lime juice, then use his mixture to coat the chicken and marinate for around 30 minutes up to 24 hours, if desired. Grill chicken until it is done through, around 3-5 minutes on each side over moderate temperature, then set aside for 5 minutes to let it cool before slicing and serving.

3.27 Grilled Tom Yum Shrimp

Prep time: 10 minutes

Cooking time: 20 minutes

Servings: 4

Ingredients:

- One pound of deveined and peeled shrimp
- Three cloves of garlic
- Two stalks of chopped and peeled lemongrass
- One thumb-sized part of galangal (or chopped and peeled ginger)
- A quarter cup of chopped cilantro
- One chili birds eye (or any other hot chili or one teaspoon of chili sauce)
- One lime (zest and juice)
- Half teaspoon of shrimp paste
- Two sliced green onions
- Two tablespoons of grated sugar palm
- Two tablespoons of fish sauce
- Two tablespoons of oil

Instructions:

In a food blender, combine the garlic, lemongrass, galangal, cilantro, lime juice, zest, chili, green onions, fish sauce, shrimp paste, oil, plus palm sugar. Place shrimp in this mixture and let it marinate for a minimum of 10 minutes. Add shrimp to skewer. Cook for around 2-3 minutes on each side on the grill until done.

3.28 Pesto Style Bbq Chicken, Tomato and Zucchini Skewers

Prep time: 10 minutes

Cooking time: 10 minutes

Servings: 4

Ingredients:

- 1 pound of skinless and boneless chicken thighs or breast
- One pound of cherry/grapes tomatoes
- 1 pound of zucchini, sliced into 1-4 to 1/2 inch thick
- 1/3 cup of basil pesto

Instructions:

Add chicken to pesto and place in a resale-able bag to marinate in the fridge. Skewer all the ingredients and grill over moderate temperature for 2-6 minutes on each side or until grilled and slightly charred.

Chapter 04: Recipes of Red Meat

This chapter will help you to learn and try the various basic varieties of recipes that are made by using red meat. It definitely consists of an infinite number of options to try regarding your particular flavor. Different kinds of red meat such as lamb, pork, beef and mutton and many more are used for grilling. All the recipes are given in detail with the particular instructions as well as ingredients.

4.1 Grilled Cabbage Steak

Prep time: 15 minutes

Cooking time: 20 minutes

Servings: 4

Ingredients:

- Extra-virgin olive oil

- One cabbage head, sliced into thick rounds

- Kosher salt

- Pinch of red pepper flakes, crushed

- Black pepper, freshly ground

- Ranch dressing used for your serving

- Cooked bacon, chopped

- Green onions, chopped

- Blue cheese in a crumbled form

Instructions:

Preheat your grill over medium-high heat. Grease the cabbage steaks using oil on both sides and season with pepper, salt, and red pepper flakes. Now, place on grill and cook it until tender for around 5 minutes per side and coat with blue cheese, bacon, and scallions. Now, the food is ready to serve.

4.2 Grilled Soy Honey Pork Chops

Prep time: 10 mins

Cooking time: 45 mins

Servings: 4

Ingredients:

- Half cup of soy sauce

- A quarter cup of honey

- Two minced cloves of garlic

- Four pork chops, boneless

- Flakes of red pepper

Instructions:

Mix together soy sauce, garlic, honey, and flakes of red pepper in a bowl, then add pork chops and cover for at least 30 minutes or up to two hours. Heat your grill over a medium-high flame and cook until seared and cooked through, 8 minutes per side. Let them cool for 5 minutes before serving.

4.3 Jalapeño Popper Burgers

Prep time: 15 mins

Cooking time: 15 mins

Servings: 4

Instructions:

- Half cup of shredded cheddar
- 4 ounce of cream cheese
- Four burger buns
- Half cup of mozzarella, shredded
- Kosher salt
- Two minced jalapeños
- Black pepper, grounded
- Half teaspoon of chili powder
- Six slices of cooked bacon, chopped
- 1 to half Angus of beef, ground

Instructions:

In a medium bowl, mix together cheddar, cream cheese, mozzarella, and jalapeños and season with salt and pepper. Cut the beef into eight large, thin pieces. Spoon about one-fourth cup of filling mixture onto the one patty, then put a second patty on top. Pinch edges of burger and re-shape it if necessary. Repeat the process with the rest of the patties and filling mixture. Then, preheat the grill to medium-high flame. Season burgers with chili powder, pepper salt. Place on grill and cook them to your liking, for around 6 minutes per side for medium. Sandwich with burger buns is ready to serve immediately.

4.4 Classic burger

Prep time: 5mins

Cooking time: 10 mins

Servings: 3

Ingredients:

- Kosher salt

- 1 pound of grounded beef

- Black pepper, grounded

- Three hamburger buns

- Three slices of cheddar cheese

- Mustard

- One tomato, sliced

- Three iceberg lettuce or leaves butter

- One red onion, sliced

- Ketchup

- Mayonnaise

Ingredients:

Shape the beef into three equally sized patties and season each patty with pepper and salt. Press the center of each burger by using fingers. Then, heat your grill or grill pan to high flame and grill for around 6 minutes; put some cheese on top of patties for around 2 to 3 minutes before the burger is finished cooking.

Heat your skillet to a medium-high heat and cook patties for around 6 minutes. If you are using cheese, top on patties 2- 3 minutes before the burger is finished cooking. This process is used for the skillet. Now, place your patties on buns and do the topping. The food is ready to serve.

4.5 BLT Burgers

Prep time: 25 mins

Cooking time: 10 mins

Servings: 4

Ingredients:

- 1 pound of halved bacon slices
- Black pepper freshly ground
- kosher salt
- 1 pound of ground beef
- 1/2 cup of mayonnaise
- Three tablespoons of chopped chives
- ½ of lemon juice
- Lettuce Butterhead, for serving
- Two sliced tomatoes

Instructions:

Preheat your oven to 400° and place a rack in the oven. Line 3 halves of bacon on the rack and place the fourth half of bacon on top of the side pieces. Then, lift the two sides of the bacon and put a 5th half bacon on the middle piece. In the end, lift the other middle slice and put the 6th slice on top of the side pieces. Repeat the rest of the process to make a second weave. Season them with pepper and bake them until the bacon is crispy. Transfer the cooked bacon to a paper towel. Let them cool for 10 minutes.

For preparing burgers, preheat your grill to medium-high heat and shape the beef into large patties. Season both the sides with pepper and salt. Grill until it is cooked for around 4 minutes per side. Stir together lemon juice, mayonnaise and chives in a bowl to make herb mayo. Now, put a bacon weave on the bottom and then spray some herb mayo. Top it with the lettuce, burger, and tomato. Serve your food immediately.

4.6 Caprese Steak

Prep time: 15 mins

Cooking time: 15 mins

Servings: 4

Ingredients:

- Three cloves of minced garlic
- Two tablespoons of olive oil extra-virgin
- Two tablespoons of honey
- One tablespoon of dried oregano
- ¾ cups of balsamic vinegar
- 4 -6-ounce filet mignon, or four large pieces of sirloin
- Two beefsteak sliced tomatoes
- kosher salt
- One tablespoon of dried thyme
- Four slices of mozzarella
- Fresh basil leaves, for serving

Instructions:

Stir together garlic, dried thyme, honey, balsamic vinegar, olive oil, and dried oregano in a bowl. Pour over the steak and let it marinate for 20 minutes. Then, Season tomatoes with pepper and salt. Heat your grill to high. Grill steak for around 4 to 5 minutes per side, and coat with tomatoes and mozzarella. Cover your grill for 2 minutes until cheese is melty. Roll with the basil before serving to your guests.

4.7 Pineapple Bun Burgers

Prep time: 10 mins

Cooking time: 10 mins

Servings: 4

Ingredients:

- 1 pound of ground beef

- Eight slices of cooked bacon

- One tablespoon of Worcestershire sauce

- Black pepper Freshly ground

- One large red onion, sliced into rings

- kosher salt

- Four slices of pepper jack

- Eight pineapple rings

- Four pieces of romaine

Instructions:

Heat your grill to medium-high. Combine Worcestershire and ground beef in a bowl. Then, season with the pepper salt and form into four patties. Grill patties, red onion, and pineapple for 3 minutes until charred. Coat the burger patties with pepper jack and cover your grill for around 1 minute. Now, roll the bottom of pineapple buns with lettuce, bacon, burger patties, and grilled onions, then top with pineapple bun and serve food to your guests.

4.8 Lime-Honey Tilapia with Corn Foil Pack

Prep time: 10 mins

Cooking time: 15 mins

Servings: 4

Ingredients:

- ¼ cup of olive oil extra-virgin
- Four fillets of tilapia
- Four thinly sliced limes
- Two tablespoons of honey
- Two tablespoons of fresh cilantro leaves
- Two ears corn, shucked
- kosher salt
- Black pepper Freshly ground

Instructions:

Heat your grill to high and cut four sheets of foil about 12" long. Roll every piece of foil with a piece of tilapia. Then, grease tilapia with the honey and coat with corn, lime, and cilantro. Spray olive oil and season with salt and pepper. Grill for 15 minutes until tilapia is cooked through and corn becomes tender. Serve your food.

4.9 Tomato Bun Sliders

Prep time: 10 mins

Cooking time: 10 mins

Servings: 6

Ingredients:

- One tablespoon of mayonnaise
- 1 pound of ground beef
- kosher salt

- Black pepper Freshly ground

- Lettuce, for serving

- Six small halved tomatoes

- One tablespoon of Worcestershire sauce

- Yellow mustard, for serving

Instructions:

Heat your grill to medium-high. Combine Worcestershire and ground beef. Then, season them with salt and pepper. Make a mixture of beef in small sliders that will fit the size of your tomatoes. Now, grill beef for 3 minutes per side. Roll with cheddar and cover grill to let melt for 1 minute. Put mayo on the bottom of the tomato bun and top with a slider patty and lettuce. Spray with mustard and coat with tomato bun. Food is ready to serve.

4.10 Grilled Pork Chops

Prep time: Half-hour

Cooking time: 10 mins

Servings: 4

Ingredients:

- ½ cup of packed cilantro stems and leaves

- Six peaches

- salt

- Three cloves of garlic

- Pepper

- A cup of fresh lime juice

- One tablespoon of lower-sodium soy sauce

- Four boneless pork chops

- ¼ tablespoon of grounded red pepper

- One tablespoon dark brown sugar

- One bunch of green onions

Instructions:

Mix cilantro, garlic, and 1/4 teaspoon freshly ground black pepper pulse until very finely grounded in a processor. Add soy sauce and pulse it to integrate. Then, put it in a large bag of plastic and add pork chops. Rub the garlic mixture on every chop, seal the bag tightly, and refrigerate up to overnight until the mixture ready to grill. In the same processor, combine sugar, lime juice, red pepper, and two peaches and now cut into pieces pulse until smooth. This can be covered and refrigerated overnight. Prepare your grill for direct grilling on medium-high heat. Then, cut remaining peaches into equal sizes and grill for 5 to 7 minutes or until grill marks appear on peaches and turning occasionally. Grill chops for 5 to 6 minutes until cooked through. Also, grill green onions for 3 minutes. Serve your food with sauce.

4.11 Beer Can Burgers

Prep time: 30-35 minutes

Cooking time: 30 minutes

Servings: 3-4 persons

Ingredients:

- One tablespoon of Worcestershire sauce

- One tablespoon of garlic powder

- Two pounds of ground beef

- One beer can

- Freshly ground black pepper

- Eight slices of bacon

- kosher salt

- Four burger buns

- Two pieces of lettuce

- Two cups of cubed cheddar

- Four slices of tomato

- One jalapeño, thinly sliced

- One onion that is thinly sliced

- Four slices of provolone

- One sliced bell pepper

Instructions:

Preheat the grill to moderate temperature. Season beef using Worcestershire plus garlic powder in a big cup. Roll into 1/2-pound balls, then form into a bowl by placing a beer can in the center. Push beef up the edges of the beer can. Season using pepper and salt after gently twisting the beer can out of the burger bowl. Wrap two pieces of bacon across the bowl. Cover with cheese plus jalapenos if using cheddar and jalapenos. Fill with onions and peppers and finish with a strip of provolone if using onions and peppers. Grill until the burger is cooked through, around 30 minutes. Serve with tomato and lettuce on buns.

4.12 Fries and Burger Foil Packs

Prep time: 10 mins

Cooking time: 15 mins

Servings: 4

Ingredients:

- 1 pound of ground beef

- One tablespoon Worcestershire sauce

- Cooking spray for foil

- One tablespoon of garlic powder

- Freshly ground black pepper

- 1 pound of frozen bag fries

- Four slices cheddar

- kosher salt

- Pickles, for serving

- Ketchup, for drizzling

- Mustard, for drizzling
- Sliced tomatoes for serving

Instructions:

Spray four aluminum foil sheets using cooking spray and heat the grill to moderate temperature. Combine the Worcestershire sauce, garlic powder and ground beef in a big mixing bowl and season using pepper and salt. Make four patties out of the mixture. Place frozen fries with each patty on an aluminum foil sheet. Fold the foil packets. Grill for around 10 minutes, open the foil packs and top the patties using cheddar. Cover the grill for 2 minutes to allow the cheese to melt. Tomatoes and pickles go on top of the sandwiches and drizzle mustard plus ketchup on top.

4.13 Jalapeño Popper Corn Dip

Prep time: 15 mins

Cooking time: 10 mins

Servings: 7-8

Ingredients:

- 1/3 cup of sour cream
- One tablespoon of garlic powder
- Two minced jalapeños
- 1 8 ounces of block cream cheese
- 1 1/2 cups of shredded Cheddar
- 1 1/2 cups of Shredded Monterey Jack
- 3 cups of corn
- kosher salt
- Eight slices of cooked bacon, chopped, plus more for garnish
- Freshly ground black pepper
- Two tablespoons of finely chopped chives
- Tortilla chips, for serving
- pinch of paprika

Instructions:

Mix together cream cheese, garlic powder, jalapenos and sour cream in a big bowl until buttery. Stir in the Monterey Jack, cheddar, corn and bacon and mix to combine everything. Season using pepper, paprika and salt to taste. Cover firmly with foil after the mixture has been transferred to the skillet. Cook over a hot grill until the mixture turns bubbly, and cheese melts. Serve hot with tortilla chips and additional cooked bacon as well as chives.

4.14 BBQ Asian Salmon

Prep time: 10 minutes

Cooking time: half an hour

Servings: 4

Ingredients:

- 1/4 cup of water

- Two tablespoons of cornstarch

- Four tablespoons of honey

- 1/4 cup of low-sodium soy sauce

- Two tablespoons of pineapple juice

- Two minced cloves of garlic

- Four salmon fillets, boneless with skin on

- Two tablespoons of rice wine vinegar

- kosher salt

- Freshly ground black pepper

- Toasted sesame seeds for garnish

- Fresh cilantro, for garnish

- Six green onions

Instructions:

In a saucepan, mix together all of the ingredients. Simmer, stirring sometimes, until the paste has thickened sufficiently to cover the spoon.

Preheat the barbecue to 375 degrees Fahrenheit. Put the salmon on the skin-side on a cedar plank board that has been soaked for around 30 minutes or onto a baking sheet lined with parchment. Season using pepper and salt. Close the cover and grill for around 20 minutes, just until it is lightly cooked through. Rub teriyaki sauce liberally over the salmon, then re-cover the grill. Grill for another 5 minutes, then turn off the heat and drizzle with additional glaze, if necessary. Sear green onions for 2 to 3 minutes on both sides directly on a warm grill surface. Serve with green onions & sesame seeds on top of the salmon.

4.15 Cheese Beer Brats

Prep time: 5 mins

Cooking time: Half-hour

Servings: 10

Ingredients:

- One sweet sliced onion
- Two minced cloves of garlic
- Ten brats
- 36 Ounce of beer
- Ten buns
- Two tablespoons of all-purpose flour
- Four Ounce for beer
- Two tablespoons of butter
- Four Ounce milk
- One tablespoon of smoked paprika
- Two tablespoons of freshly chopped chives
- Eight Ounce of shredded Cheddar

Instructions:

Bring the onion, garlic and beer to a boil in a big pot. Simmer the brats in the liquid for around 15 minutes, then extract them from the liquid and place them on a hot grill. Grill each side for around

6 minutes until cooked through. In the meantime, make the cheese sauce as follows: Melt the butter in a medium frying pan over moderate heat, then whisk in the flour. Cook for one minute. Slowly pour in the beer plus milk while continually stirring the flour mixture. Keep stirring over moderate heat for another 3 minutes or until the solution has thickened. Take the pan off the flame and stir in the cheese. Mix until cheese melts, and the sauce turns smooth; add the brats in buns and pour with cheese sauce. On top, sprinkle chives and smoked paprika.

4.16 Butter Lemon Salmon Foil Packs

Prep time: 10 mins

Cooking time: 12 mins

Servings: 4

Ingredients:

- Two minced cloves of garlic
- kosher salt
- Two thinly sliced zucchinis
- Freshly ground pepper
- Six salmon fillets
- Four tablespoons butter, divided
- Two thinly sliced lemons
- Fresh parsley, for garnish
- Four sprigs thyme
- white wine

Instructions:

Preheat the grill to moderate temperature. On a smooth surface, place a big piece of foil. Add one layer of diced zucchini and a spritz of garlic. Season using pepper and salt, then scatter a few slices of lemon. Season using pepper and salt and finish with a fillet of salmon. Cover the salmon fillet with a tbsp. of butter. Place a thyme sprig on top of the salmon, then add a little trickle of white wine over it. To secure the packet, flip the foil in half and then up the sides. To produce four packets, repeat for the rest of the ingredients. Position the packets on the grill and cook for around12 minutes, or until the zucchini is soft and the salmon is done completely. Serve warm, garnished with parsley.

4.17 Cheesesteak Philly Foil Packs

Prep time: 10 mins

Cooking time: 15 mins

Servings: 4

Ingredients:

- Two thinly sliced bell peppers
- 1/2 thinly sliced onion
- 1 pound of flank steak, thinly sliced
- Two minced cloves of garlic
- Two tablespoons of olive oil
- kosher salt
- Two tablespoons of Italian seasoning
- Freshly ground black pepper
- Chopped fresh parsley for garnish
- Four slices of provolone

Instructions:

Preheat the grill to moderate temperature. Toss the peppers, steak, onion, Italian seasoning, olive oil and garlic in a big bowl and season using pepper and salt. Fill foil packs with the steak blend.

Fold the packets and grill for around 10 minutes. Open the bags, top using provolone, and cover the grill for 2 minutes to melt the cheese. Serve garnished with parsley.

4.18 Steak Taco

Prep time: 15 mins

Cooking time: 10 mins

Servings: 1

Ingredients:

- 1/2 chopped jalapeño
- 1 cup of chopped fresh cilantro
- Two cloves of minced garlic
- One tablespoon of ground cumin
- 1/4 cup of vegetable oil
- 1/2 tablespoon of kosher salt
- 1/3 cup of lime juice
- 3/4 pound of sirloin steak, cut into 1" pieces
- Lime wedges, for serving
- Two ears corn and sliced into 1" thick pieces
- One small red onion and cut into 1" pieces
- one avocado and cut into chunks
- Two flour tortillas and cut into triangles
- Hot sauce, for serving

Instructions:

To make the marinade, follow these steps: Add the garlic, cilantro, jalapeño, lime juice, vegetable oil and cumin in a medium sized bowl and season using pepper and salt. Set aside half of the marinade and apply the other half to the steak. Toss until it is evenly coated. Toss corn, avocado, tortillas and red onion with the leftover marinade in a big mixing bowl. Preheat the grill to a high temperature. Grill for around 8 minutes after skewering the kebabs. Present with a squeeze of lime and a dash of hot sauce.

4.19 Broccoli and Beef Kebabs

Prep time: 20 minutes

Cooking time: 15 minutes

Servings: 4

Ingredients:

- 1/4 cup of brown sugar
- Juice of 2 limes or one if large, plus more for serving
- 1/3 cup of low-sodium soy sauce
- One tablespoon of ground ginger
- Two tablespoons of olive oil
- 1 pound of sirloin steak, cut into cubes
- Freshly ground black pepper
- 2 cups of broccoli florets
- Green onions, for garnish

Instructions:

Preheat the grill to moderate temperature. Whisk together brown sugar, soy sauce, lime juice, ginger and lime juice in a tiny bowl. Toss the steak in the mixture until it is evenly coated. Place at least for around 15 minutes and up to 2 hours to marinate in the fridge. Mix olive oil with broccoli florets in a separate dish. Season the broccoli and steak using pepper. Grill for around 8 minutes, rotating regularly until steak turns medium. Serve with a squeeze of lime and green onions on top.

4.20 Fajita Steak Skewers

Prep time: 15 mins

Cooking time: 10 mins

Servings: 8

Ingredients:

- 1 pack small of flour tortillas and torn into large pieces
- kosher salt
- 1 pound of sirloin steak and cut into large cubes
- Eight skewers and soaked in water for 20 minutes
- One bunch of scallions and cut into thirds
- Four large bell peppers and cut into large pieces
- Olive oil Extra-virgin, for drizzling
- Freshly ground black pepper

Instructions:

Preheat your grill to medium-high. Skewer scallions, steak, folded tortillas and peppers. Spray with olive oil and season with the salt and pepper. Grill for around 7 minutes, flipping occasionally until the steak is medium-rare and vegetables are tender and slightly charred.

4.21 Grilled Steak with Guacamole and Blistered Tomatoes

Prep time: 10 mins

Cooking time: 20 mins

Servings: 4

Ingredients:

- One tablespoon of coriander
- One and a half pound of skirt steak
- Two tablespoons of cumin
- kosher salt

- Three tablespoons of olive oil

- Two minced garlic cloves

- Two tablespoons of fresh chopped cilantro

- Four tablespoons of lime juice

- 3/4 cup of halved red grape like tomatoes

- Three diced avocados

- Two tablespoons of finely chopped red onion

- 1/2 tablespoon of crushed red pepper flakes

- 3/4 cup of halved yellow grape like tomatoes

- Freshly crushed black pepper

Instructions:

Put the steak into the shallow baking dish. Take a bowl and stir together coriander, two tablespoons of olive oil, cumin, garlic, and two tablespoons of lime juice. Put this mixture over the steak then turning to the coat, and marinate it for 10 minutes. In a bowl, mix together onion, avocado, cilantro, remaining two tablespoons of lime juice, and red pepper flakes until lumpy and then season with the salt to make guacamole.

Mix your tomatoes with the remaining one tablespoon of olive oil and then season with pepper and salt. Heat your grill pan on medium to high heat. Grill tomatoes for 4 minutes until blistered, then remove your tomatoes and then increase the heat to high. Now, add steaks to your grill and then season it with pepper and salt. Then, grill for 3 minutes on each side for medium to rare, then let rest for 5 minutes. Slice steak thinly against your grain. Coat with tomatoes which are blistered and cilantro, and serve with some guacamole to your guests.

4.22 Grilled Steaks with French Potato Salad and Chive Garlic Butter

Prep time: 20 mins

Cooking time: 15 mins

Servings: 4

Ingredients:

- 1 1/2 pound of small red potatoes
- Four tablespoons of unsalted butter at room temperature
- Three tablespoons of minced chives, divided
- 1/2 small minced shallot
- One small minced garlic clove
- kosher salt
- Freshly ground black pepper
- One tablespoon of Dijon mustard
- Two tablespoons of red wine vinegar
- 1/4 cup of olive oil extra-virgin
- Two tablespoons of finely chopped fresh parsley
- Two tablespoons of finely chopped fresh basil
- Two green onions, halved lengthwise and white and light green parts thinly sliced
- Two 10-ounce NY strip steaks halved

Instructions:

Bring the medium pot of water to boil and add potatoes. Boil for 20 minutes, then drain. When cool enough to handle, cut them into quarters. Stir together one tablespoon of chives, butter, shallot, and garlic. Season with the salt and pepper in a bowl. Cover and place in the refrigerator until ready to use. Stir together red wine vinegar and Dijon mustard, then slowly stir in olive oil and season with salt and pepper. Then, add in potatoes, two tablespoons of chives, basil, green onions, parsley, and stir gently to combine well. Season with pepper and salt. Heat lightly the oiled grill pan over high heat, and season the steaks with salt and pepper. Grill for 3 minutes per side for the medium-rare. Put a dollop of chive butter on every steak and let rest a few minutes, then serve to your guests with potato salad.

4.23 Steak Bbq Skewers with Chimichurri

Prep time: 20 mins

Cooking time: 10 mins

Servings: 4

Ingredients:

- One third cup of fresh parsley
- 1/3 cup of fresh basil
- Freshly ground black pepper
- 1/3 cup of fresh cilantro
- One tablespoon vinegar of red wine
- One minced garlic clove
- One orange pepper and cut into 1 1/2 pieces
- One minced shallot
- Juice of half lemon
- 1/2 tablespoon of crushed flakes of red pepper
- 1/2 cup of olive oil extra-virgin, divided
- One red onion and cut into one and a half chunks
- kosher salt
- One red pepper and cut into one and a half pieces
- One yellow pepper and cut into one and a half pieces
- 1 1/2 pound of sirloin steak

Instructions:

Soak twelve skewers made with wood in water for about 10 minutes then in a food processor or blender, pulse together basil, cilantro, parsley, garlic, vinegar, crushed flakes of red pepper, shallot, two tablespoons of olive oil and lemon juice. With the running motor, add a quarter cup of more olive oil until it is smooth well, then season it with the pepper and salt.

Thread steak, onion and peppers onto soaked skewers and then make them sturdy by using two skewers for each kebab. Arrange your skewers on the platter and then season kindly with the salt and pepper. Spray with the remaining two tablespoons of olive oil, then flipping skewers to coat. Grill your skewers over some high heat for 10-12 minutes, flipping after few minutes to brown from all sides, or wait for the interior temperature of the steak to reaches 145° for medium to rare. Let it sit for 5 minutes and then serve skewers with some couscous and chimichurri. Enjoy your food.

4.24 Grilled Tilapia

Prep time: 10 mins

Cooking time: 10 mins

Servings: 3

Ingredients:

- 1/4 small thinly sliced red onion

- Three tablespoons of olive oil extra-virgin, divided

- Freshly ground black pepper

- Two tablespoons of red wine vinegar

- Kosher salt

- 3 -8 ounce of tilapia filets

- Two tablespoons of fresh oregano leaves

- 1/2 cup of grape tomatoes

Instructions:

Preheat your grill to medium-high heat and take a medium bowl; stir two tablespoons of olive oil with the red wine vinegar. Then, add oregano and red onion and season with pepper and salt. Grease tilapia with the remaining olive oil and season with pepper and salt. Put your filets and grape tomatoes on the preheated grill. Cook your grape tomatoes for around 4 minutes until it blistered and soft. Grill your tilapia for 4 minutes until the edges are opaque and the flesh lets go easily from the grill. Remove the fish onto the serving plate. Roll grilled tomatoes with the vinegar mixture and spoon over your filets. Serve your food immediately.

4.25 Grilled Halibut

Prep time: 5 mins

Cooking time: 15 mins

Servings: 4

Ingredients:

- Two tablespoons of olive oil extra-virgin
- Kosher salt
- 4-6 ounce of halibut steaks
- Freshly ground black pepper
- Kosher salt
- One diced mango
- Juice of 1 lime
- 1/2 diced red onion
- One minced jalapeno
- One finely chopped red pepper
- One tablespoon of freshly chopped cilantro
- Freshly ground black pepper

Instructions:

Preheat your grill to medium-high and grease halibut by using oil on both sides, then season with the pepper and salt. Grill halibut for 5 minutes until cooked through. Mix together all the salsa ingredients in a bowl and season with salt and pepper. Serve your salsa over the halibut.

4.26 Lime Honey Tilapia with Corn Foil Pack

Prep time: 10 mins

Cooking time: 10 mins

Servings: 4

Ingredients:

- 1/4 cup of olive oil extra-virgin
- kosher salt
- Two tablespoons of honey
- Four thinly sliced limes
- Four fillets of tilapia
- Two chucked ears corn
- Two tablespoons of fresh cilantro leaves
- Freshly ground black pepper

Instructions:

Heat your grill to high and cut four sheets of foil about 12 long. Roll each piece of the foil with a piece of tilapia. Grease tilapia with the honey and top with corn, lime, and cilantro. Then, spray olive oil and season it with salt and pepper. Grill for 15 minutes until tilapia is cooked through and corn tender.

4.27 Grilled Mahi Steak with Corn Salsa and Avocado

Prep time: 20 mins

Cooking time: 10 mins

Servings: 4

Ingredients:

- Two tablespoons of olive oil
- Four Mahi fillets that are thawed
- Two teaspoons of ground cumin

- Half teaspoon salt

- Two teaspoons of chili powder

- 1/4 teaspoon of pepper

- One small poblano pepper is seeded and also chopped

- Two fresh ears of corn that are shucked and also cob are removed

- One ripe firm avocado into cubed

- 1/3 cup of chopped onion

- A quarter teaspoon of pepper

- Half cup of red pepper which is chopped

- Three tablespoons of olive oil

- One tablespoon of vinegar

- One tablespoon of sugar

- Half teaspoon of salt

Instructions:

For making the Salsa, add all of the ingredients to a bowl. Chill it while the fish is about to grill. For making Mahi heat outdoor or indoor grill mild high. In a small bowl, combine cumin, olive oil, pepper and salt, chili powder. Brush it onto your Mahi fillets that are not cooked. Grill this for about four minutes from each side (that depends on the thickness of your fillet) until cooked to an internal temperature of about 145 degrees F, and fish easily flakes. Serve this with Salsa.

Chapter 05: Seafood recipes

This chapter will introduce you to the vast and basic recipes containing a variety of ingredients regarding grilling of seafood which may include recipes of shrimps, salmon, prawns and codfish. These seafood recipes are exclusively for those who are searching for healthy and clean food.

5.1 Grilled Shrimp Tacos with Sriracha Slaw

Prep time: 10 minutes

Cooking time: 30 minutes

Servings: 4

Ingredients:

- Three tablespoons cilantro, chopped

- A quarter cup of olive oil, extra-virgin

- Four tortillas, size should be medium

- Juice of three lemons

- Black pepper, grounded

- Kosher salt

- 1-ounce shrimp, peeled

- A quarter cup of mayonnaise

- Quarter head of red shredded cabbage

- One tablespoon of sriracha

Instructions:

Stir together cilantro, olive oil, and 1/3 of the lime juice and season them with pepper and salt. Now, add shrimp to a baking dish and pour over the mixture. Roll until completely coated with the mixture and let marinate for around 20 minutes. Then, take a bowl and roll cabbage with mayo, remaining Sriracha and lime juice. Season it with salt and heat the grill to a high flame. Skewer the shrimp and grill for around 3 minutes. Also, grill tortillas for 1 minute per side. Food is ready to serve.

5.2 Gilled Fish Tacos

Prep time: 20 mins

Cooking time: 10 mins

Servings: 4

Ingredients:

- Three tablespoons of olive oil extra-virgin

- 1 1/2 pound of cod or other flaky white fish

- Juice of 1 lime

- One tablespoon of paprika

- 1/2 tablespoon of ground cumin

- Two tablespoons of chili powder

- Freshly ground black pepper

- 1/2 tablespoon of cayenne pepper

- 1/2 tablespoon of vegetable oil

- Kosher salt

- Eight corn of tortillas

- 1 cup of corn kernels

- Lime wedges, for serving

- Sour cream, for serving

- 1/4 cup of mayonnaise

- One diced avocado

- Juice of 1 lime

- One tablespoon of honey

- 2 cups of shredded purple cabbage

- Two tablespoons of freshly chopped cilantro

- One minced jalapeño

Instructions:

Stir together lime juice, olive oil, cumin, paprika, chili powder and cayenne in a bowl. Add cod and roll until evenly coated. Let marinate for 15 minutes.

Take a bowl and make the slaw, so stir together cilantro, mayonnaise, honey and lime juice in corn, cabbage, and jalapeño. Season with the salt and pepper. In a non-stick skillet over medium-high heat, heat the vegetable oil and remove cod from the marinade. Now season both sides of each filet with the salt and pepper. Add fish and cook for 3 to 5 minutes on each side until opaque. Let rest for 5 minutes before flaking with a fork. Serve your fish over grilled tortillas with corn slaw and avocado. In the end, squeeze lime juice on top of tacos and garnish it with sour cream. Enjoy your food

5.3 Grilled Shrimp Packets with Foil

Prep time: 10 mins

Cooking time: 15 mins

Servings: 4

Ingredients:

- 1 1/2 pound of large peeled and deveined shrimp

- Two cloves of minced garlic

- two smoked thinly sliced andouille sausages

- two ears corn, each cut crosswise into four pieces

- one pound of red bliss potatoes, chopped into pieces

- two tablespoons of olive oil extra-virgin

- one tablespoon of Old Bay

- Kosher salt

- Black pepper freshly ground

- two tablespoons of freshly chopped parsley

- one lemon, sliced into thin wedges

- four tablespoons of butter

Instructions:

Preheat your grill on high heat, or you can preheat the oven to about 425° and cut four foil sheets of 12 inches long. Divide garlic, shrimp, sausage, potatoes, and corn evenly all over your foil sheets. Spray with oil and then add seasoning of Old Bay and season it to taste with pepper and salt. Roll it gently to mix and coat each mixture with lemon, parsley, and a tablespoon of butter. Fold foil packets in crosswise manner over shrimp & cover completely. Roll the bottom and top edges. Put foil packets over grill & cook for about 15 to 20 minutes until cooked through, or transfer it to the oven and bake for 20 minutes.

5.4 Lime Cilantro Shrimp Foil Packs

Prep time: 10 mins

Cooking time: 10 mins

Servings: 4

Ingredients:

- Three ears corn quartered

- One zucchini and cut into half-moons

- 1 pound of medium shrimp, peeled and deveined

- Two minced cloves of garlic

- One tablespoon of crushed red pepper flakes

- Two tablespoons of freshly chopped cilantro

- Two tablespoons of ground cumin

- Olive oil for drizzling

- Freshly ground black pepper

- Two limes, sliced into rounds

- kosher salt

- Two tablespoons of butter

Instructions:

Combine the corn, shrimp, zucchini, cumin, garlic, cilantro and pepper flakes in a big bowl. Drizzle using olive oil, season using pepper and salt, and mix until well combined. Place four sheets of foil on the board. Distribute the shrimp mixture among the foil sheets and finish with lime slices and a touch of butter. Seal the packs. Preheat the grill to a high temperature. Position the shrimp packs on the grill and cook for around 10 minutes or until the shrimp become pink.

5.5 Grilled Boil Shrimp

Prep time: 45 mins

Cooking time: 15 mins

Servings: 8

Ingredients:

- Two minced cloves of garlic

- Two smoked thinly sliced andouille sausages

- 1 1/2 pound of large shrimp, peeled and deveined

- Two ears of corn which are cut crosswise into four pieces

- Two tablespoons of olive oil

- Three tablespoons of Old Bay seasoning, divided

- 1 pound of red potatoes that are chopped into 1 inch pieces

- Four tablespoons of butter, melted

- kosher salt

- One lemon, cut into tinny wedges

- Freshly crushed black pepper

- Two tablespoons of fresh chopped parsley leaves, divided

Instructions:

Preheat your grill to moderate temperature. In a medium frying pan, place the potatoes, add water and use salt to season. Boil the water, then reduce to low heat and simmer until the potatoes are soft. In the meantime, combine the shrimp, garlic, olive oil, two teaspoons of Old Bay, and one tablespoon of parsley in a moderate-sized bowl. Toss the shrimp in the mixture until it's evenly covered. Place aside to marinate for around 15 minutes. Combine corn, melted butter, cooked potatoes, one teaspoon Old Bay, plus one tablespoon parsley in another medium-sized bowl. Using metal skewers, thread shrimp, potatoes, lemon, sausage, plus corn. Grill skewers for around 4-5 minutes overall, turning halfway through until shrimp is translucent and lemon is grilled.

5.6 Shrimp Cajun Kebabs

Prep time: 5 mins

Cooking time: 5 mins

Servings: 4-6

Ingredients:

- Two tablespoons of olive oil

- One tablespoon of kosher salt

- One tablespoon oregano

- 1 pound of shrimp

- One tablespoon of cayenne

- One tablespoon of garlic powder

- One tablespoon of paprika

- One tablespoon of onion powder

- Two lemons cut thinly crosswise

Instructions:

Preheat the grill to moderate temperature. Prepare a Cajun spice blend. In a tiny bowl, combine cayenne, salt, paprika, onion powder, oregano and garlic powder. Stir everything together using a fork until it's almost smooth. Toss shrimp with olive oil in a medium-sized bowl. Add the spice blend and toss the shrimp until it is finely covered. Use metal skewers to thread the shrimp and lemon. Grill skewers for around 4-5 minutes overall, turning halfway through until shrimp is translucent and lemon is grilled.

5.7 Grilled Hot Shot Salmon

Prep time: 10 mins

Cooking time: 3 hours and 10 mins

Servings: 4

Ingredients:

- 1 cup of sriracha

- Juice of 2 lemons

- 1/4 cup of honey

- Four 6-ounce skin-on salmon fillets

- Chopped fresh chives for garnishing

Instructions:

Stir together honey, lemon juice and Sriracha in a bowl. Reserve 1/2 cup of marinade for basting salmon after grilling. Then, add salmon to a large Ziploc bag or in a baking dish and pour it over marinade. Let marinate for 3 hours or up to overnight in the refrigerator.

When the marinade is ready to grill, heat your grill to high and oil grates of the grill and add salmon, then baste with the marinade and grill for 5 minutes per side until cooked through. Now, baste with the reserved marinade and garnish with chives. Your food is ready to serve.

5.8 Shrimp Pesto Skewers

Prep time: 15 mins

Cooking time: 10 mins

Servings: 8

Ingredients:

- kosher salt

- 1 pound of medium or large frozen deveined, thawed shrimp

- 1/2 cup of pesto

- Freshly ground black pepper

- 3 thinly sliced lemons

- Eight skewers that soaked in water 20 minutes

- Olive oil Extra virgin, for drizzling

Instructions:

Preheat your grill to medium-high. Skewer shrimp and the lemon slice. Spray with the olive oil and season with pepper and salt. Grill for around 4 to 5 minutes, occasionally flipping, until shrimp is opaque and the lemons are slightly charred. Brush with the pesto and serve your food.

5.9 Shrimp Bbq Tostadas with Cabbage Slaw and Guacamole

Prep time: 15 mins

Cooking time: 15 mins

Servings: 4

Ingredients:

- Three ripe diced avocados

- 24 medium peeled and deveined shrimp

- 8 6 corn of tortillas

- 1/4 cup of finely shredded red cabbage

- One small minced shallot

- 1/2 tablespoon of cayenne

- Three tablespoons of freshly chopped cilantro

- Kosher salt

- Seven tablespoons of lime juice, divided

- Two tablespoons of cumin

- 1/4 cup of olive oil extra-virgin, divided

- 3/4 cup of finely shredded carrots (1 large carrot)

- Lime wedges, for serving

- Freshly ground black pepper

- Cilantro leaves, for serving

Instructions:

Preheat your grill or oven to 400°.

Grease 2 baking sheets by using canola oil spray and arrange the four tortillas on each sheet. Spray more oil on tortillas, then bake for around 8 minutes until golden crisp and brown. Mash together shallot, three tablespoons of lime juice, avocados, cilantro in a bowl. And season with the salt. Then, stir together cumin, two tablespoons of olive oil, cayenne, and two tablespoons of lime juice in a bowl. Add shrimp and roll lightly to coat, then season lightly with salt and pepper. Grill shrimp for around 3 minutes per side over medium-high heat or until bright pink and cooked. Roll carrot and cabbage with the remaining two tablespoons of lime juice and two tablespoons of olive oil in a bowl. Now, season with salt and pepper.

Arrange tostadas on a flat work surface and spread with the guacamole. Top with shrimp, slaw, and cilantro leaves and serve with lime.

5.10 Cod Grilled Tacos with Chipotle Crema

Prep time: 20 min

Cooking time: 10 min

Servings: 4

Ingredients:

- 1/2 tablespoon cumin
- 1 ounce of cod
- One tablespoon of Old Bay seasoning
- Juice of 1 lime, divided
- 1/2 tablespoon of chili powder
- One tablespoon of honey
- Four tablespoons of olive oil extra-virgin, divided
- 2 cups of finely sliced red cabbage
- Two tablespoons of adobo sauce from a can of chipotle peppers
- One tablespoon of lime zest
- Kosher salt
- 1/2 cup of Greek yogurt
- One tablespoon red wine vinegar
- 1/4 cups of Cilantro leaves
- 8 6 corn warmed tortillas
- Freshly ground black pepper
- One thinly sliced avocado
- Lime wedges, for serving

Instructions:

Put cod in a shallow glass of baking dish. Stir together Old Bay, chili powder, honey, cumin, three tablespoons of olive oil, and three tablespoons of lime juice. Then, put this mixture over the cod, flip it to coat, and let marinate for 10 minutes. Stir together lime zest, adobo sauce, Greek yogurt, and the remaining one tablespoon of lime juice in a bowl, then season with pepper and salt. Now, heat a lightly oiled grill pan over the medium-high heat and season your cod with pepper and salt. Grill the cod for 4 minutes per side or until flaky and cooked. Flake fish and transfer it to a bowl.

Roll cabbage, remaining one tablespoon of olive oil, and vinegar in a bowl and season with the salt. Serve your cod in corn tortillas that are layered with marinated red cabbage, avocados, and a spray of adobo crema. Sprinkle with the cilantro and serve this with lime.

5.11 Grilled Spicy Shrimp

Prep time: 5 mins

Cooking time: 10 mins

Servings: 8

Ingredients:

- 1/4 cups of lime juice

- Four minced garlic cloves

- Two tablespoons of low-sodium soy sauce

- One tablespoon of chili garlic sauce or Sriracha

- 1/4 cup of olive oil extra-virgin

- 2 pounds of shrimp, peeled and deveined

- Three tablespoons of honey

- Lime wedges, for the serving

- 1/4 cups freshly chopped cilantro for garnish

Instructions:

Stir together olive oil, soy sauce, garlic, lime juice, honey, and chili sauce. At the same time, grilling reserve 1/4 cup of marinade for greasing onto shrimp. In a bowl, roll your shrimp with the remaining marinade. Then, preheat your grill or grill pan and thread shrimp onto the skewers. Grill shrimp for 3 minutes on each side until pink and opaque; also grease with reserved 1/4 cup of the marinade before and after each turn. Garnish it with the cilantro and serve warm with the lime wedges.

5.12 Shrimp Pineapple Skewers

Prep time: 15 mins

Cooking time: 20 mins

Servings: 4

Ingredients:

- Three tablespoons of olive oil
- 3 cups of cubed pineapple
- 1 pound of peeled and deveined shrimp
- Three tablespoons of sweet chili sauce
- Two minced cloves of garlic
- Two tablespoons of toasted sesame oil crushed red pepper flakes
- 1/2 tablespoon crushed red pepper flakes
- Toasted sesame seeds for garnish
- Thinly sliced green onions for garnish
- Kosher salt
- Lime wedges, for serving

Ingredients:

Preheat your grill to medium heat and put your wooden skewers in water to soak. Alternatively, skewering pineapple and shrimp all until all are used, then put them on a large baking sheet. Combine all the ingredients like sesame oil, olive oil, garlic, chili sauce, ginger, and red pepper flakes and season with the salt. Stir until all combined and grease all over the skewers. Put skewers on your grill and cook for around 4 to 6 minutes, turning once, until shrimp is cooked through. Garnish with the sesame seeds and green onions before serving to your guests.

5.13 Grilled Fish

Prep time: 5 mins

Cooking time: 10 mins

Servings: 4

Ingredients:

- 1/4 tablespoon of cayenne pepper
- One tablespoon of chili powder
- One tablespoon of dried oregano
- Freshly ground black pepper
- Kosher salt
- ½ thick fillet skin-on white fish, such as bass or cod
- Lime wedges, for the serving

Instructions:

Heat your grill to high and stir together oregano, chili powder, and cayenne, then season with salt and pepper. Season your all fish with the spice mixture. Cook for 8 to 10 minutes skin-side down and covered until entirely opaque throughout. Flip and cook for 2 to 3 minutes more, until opaque throughout.

5.14 Grilled Lemony Salmon

Prep time: 10 mins

Cooking time: 10 mins

Servings: 4

Ingredients:

- olive oil Extra-virgin for greasing
- 4 6 ounces of skin-on salmon fillets
- kosher salt
- Two sliced lemons

- Freshly ground black pepper

- Two tablespoons of butter

Instructions:

Heat the grill to high and grease salmon by using oil and season with pepper and salt. Then, add lemon slices and salmon grill for 5 minutes on each side until your salmon is cooked through and the lemons are charred. Remove the heat and add a pat of butter to your salmon right, and coat with grilled lemons. Serve your food immediately.

5.15 Lime Cilantro Bbq Salmon

Prep time: 5 mins

Cooking time: 20 mins

Servings: 4

Ingredients:

- Kosher salt

- Freshly ground black pepper

- 4-6 ounce of salmon fillets

- Four tablespoons of butter

- 1/4 cup of honey

- Two minced garlic cloves

- 1/2 cup of lime juice

Instructions:

Season your salmon with salt and pepper and heat the grill, and place salmon on grill flesh side down. Cook for 8 minutes, then flip it and cook the other side of salmon for 6 minutes more until salmon is cooked through. Let it rest for 5 minutes. In a saucepan over the medium heat, add garlic, lime juice, butter, and honey.

Then, stir until your butter is melted and all the ingredients are combined. Turn off the heat and add cilantro. Now, pour the sauce over your salmon and serve hot.

5.16 Bbq Salmon with Pineapple Salsa

Prep time: 10 mins

Cooking time: 15 mins

Servings: 4

Ingredients:

- One tablespoon of honey

- Freshly ground black pepper

- Juice of 3 limes, divided

- Two tablespoons of olive oil extra-virgin

- 4 6 ounces of skin-on salmon fillets

- 1/4 chopped red onion

- One tablespoon of chopped fresh cilantro

- 1 1/2 cup of chopped pineapple

- kosher salt

Instructions:

Make sauce take a large bowl, and stir together honey, juice of 2 limes, and olive oil. Heat your grill to high and add salmon grease your salmon with honey-lime sauce, and grill for 5 to 6 minutes until salmon cooked through. Make pineapple salsa combine lime juice, pineapple, onion, and cilantro and season with the salt and pepper. Serve your salmon warm with salsa.

5.17 Sweet Lime-Chilli Grilled Salmon

Prep time: 10 mins

Cooking time: 3 hours and 10 mins

Servings: 4

Ingredients:

- 1/4 cup of low-sodium soy sauce

- 1 cup of sweet chili sauce

- Juice of 2 limes

- Green onions, for garnish

- 4 6 ounces of skin-on salmon fillets

- Lime wedges, for serving

Instructions:

Stir together lime juice, sweet chili sauce, and soy sauce in a bowl to make the marinade. Reserve 1/2 cup of marinade for basting your salmon after grilling. Then, add your salmon to a large bag or baking dish and pour over the marinade. Let marinate it in the refrigerator for at least 3 hours

and up to overnight. When the salmon is ready to grill, heat the grill to high. Then, grease the grill grates and add salmon. Baste with the marinade and grill for 5 minutes until cooked through. Baste with the reserved marinade and garnish with the green onions. Serve your grilled salmon with limes to your guests.

5.18 Grilled Hot Shot Salmon

Prep time: 10 mins

Cooking time: 3 hours and 10 mins

Servings: 4

Ingredients:

- 1/4 cup of honey

- 1 cup of sriracha

- Juice of 2 lemons

- Chopped fresh chives for garnish

- 4 6 ounces of skin-on salmon fillets

Instructions:

Stir together honey, Sriracha, and lemon juice in a bowl to make the marinade. Reserve 1/2 cup of marinade for basting your salmon after grilling. Then, add salmon to a Ziploc bag or a baking dish and put over the marinade. Let them marinate in the refrigerator for 3 hours or up to overnight. When it is ready to grill, heat your grill to high. Grease the grill grates with oil and add salmon, then baste with the marinade and grill for 5 minutes until cooked through. Garnish with the chives serve the food immediately.

5.19 Grilled Salmon with Lime Asparagus Packed in Foil

Prep time: 10 mins

Cooking time: 10 mins

Servings: 4

Ingredients:

- 4 -6 ounce of skin-on salmon fillets
- Four tablespoons of butter, divided
- 20 trimmed asparagus spears
- Freshly ground black pepper
- Two sliced lemons
- kosher salt
- Torn fresh dill for garnish

Instructions:

Put two pieces of your foil on a flat surface. Then, place five spears of asparagus on the foil and coat with a salmon fillets, one tablespoon of butter, and two slices of lemon. Loosely wrap your fillets, repeat with the rest of the ingredients until you have a total of four packets. Heat your grill on high and add packets of foil to grill and grill for 10 minutes until the salmon is cooked through and the asparagus is tender. Garnish with dill and serve to your guests.

5.20 Sea Salmon Skewers

Prep time: 10 mins

Cooking time: 10 mins

Servings: 4

Ingredients:

- Three sliced lemons
- Torn fresh dill for garnish

- kosher salt

- 1 pound of salmon fillets, preferably wild, and cut into two pieces

- Freshly ground black pepper

- olive oil Extra-virgin, for greasing

Instructions:

Heat your grill to high and skewer salmon and lemon slices, then grease with olive oil and season all with salt and pepper. Now, grill skewers for 6 to 8 minutes until salmon is cooked through flipping once. Garnish with the dill and serve immediately.

5.21 Butter Lemon Salmon Packed in Foil

Prep time: 10 mins

Cooking time: 10 mins

Servings: 6

Ingredients:

- kosher salt

- Two cloves of minced garlic

- Freshly ground pepper

- Two thinly sliced zucchinis

- Two thinly sliced lemons

- Four tablespoons of butter, divided

- Four sprigs thyme

- Six salmon fillets

- white wine

- Fresh parsley, for garnish

Instructions:

Preheat your grill to medium-high. Put a large piece of foil on a flat surface. Then, coat with a single layer of sliced zucchini and scatter some garlic on the top.

Season with the salt and pepper, then put a few lemon slices down. Coat with a salmon fillet and season with more of salt and pepper. Put a tablespoon of butter on top of your salmon fillet and add a sprig of thyme, then pour a small splash of white wine over the salmon. Fold your foil in half, then fold up the edges to seal the packet of foil. Repeat this process with the rest of the ingredients to make four packets. Now, place packets on your grill and cook for 10 to 12 minutes until the salmon is cooked through and your zucchini is tender. Garnish with the parsley and serve warm.

5.22 Party Style Boiled Shrimp

Prep time: 40 mins

Cooking time: 15 mins

Servings: 8

Ingredients:

- Two cloves of garlic which is minced
- One and a half-pound of large shrimp, which is peeled and deveined
- Two andouille sausages, smoked and thinly sliced
- One pound of bliss red potatoes which is chopped into one inch pieces
- Two ears corn cut crosswise into four pieces
- Two tablespoons of olive oil which is extra-virgin
- One lemon which is sliced into thinly sliced wedges
- Three teaspoons of Old Bay seasoning which is divided
- Four tablespoons of butter which is melted
- Black pepper
- kosher salt
- Two tablespoons of freshly chopped leaves of parsley which are divided

Instructions:

Heat the grill to mild-high. Add some potatoes to a medium-sized saucepan, add some water and salt. Boil water and boil until potatoes are tender. In a medium-sized bowl meanwhile, add olive oil, shrimp, 2 tsp. Old Bay garlic, and one tablespoon parsley. Toss your shrimp until it is properly coated and let it marinate for about fifteen minutes. In another medium-sized bowl, add some cooked potatoes, corn, and melted butter, one teaspoon of Old Bay and one tablespoon of parsley. Thread your shrimp, potatoes, lemon, corn and sausage onto the metal skewers (or you can use wooden skewers that were soaked for about 20 minutes). Grill your skewers until the shrimp is non-transparent and lemon is burnt and blackened, about four to five minutes in total, flipping it once halfway.

5.23 Gazpacho Tomato Bbq Shrimp with Avocado

Prep time: 20 mins

Cooking time: 5 mins

Servings: 4

Ingredients:

- One English cucumber halved lengthwise, peeled, roughly chopped, and seeded
- One and a half-pound of red heirloom tomatoes that are roughly chopped and cored
- ¼ of red onion, which is finely chopped
- Two cloves of garlic, divided and minced
- 1/3 cup of fresh cilantro, which is finely chopped
- 3/4 teaspoon of divided and crushed red pepper flakes
- Five tablespoons of olive oil
- Half diced avocado
- Three tablespoons of sherry vinegar
- kosher salt
- One tablespoon of lemon juice
- 12 shrimp which are cleaned with tails
- Freshly crushed black pepper
- One and a half teaspoon of ground cumin

Instructions:

In a bowl, mix together cucumber, tomatoes, cilantro, red onion, quarter teaspoon red pepper flakes, one clove garlic, four tablespoons olive oil, and sherry vinegar, and season with some pepper and salt. Add ½ tomato mixture in the blender and then blend until it is smooth and then pour it into a clean bowl and then blend the remains of the tomato mixture and then add to gazpacho and then taste and season with salt and pepper, and then place it in the refrigerator to cool until it is ready to serve. In a big bowl, add cumin, lemon juice, shrimp, remaining one clove of garlic and one tablespoon of olive oil, stir it to combine and then season with pepper and salt. Heat the grill pan on medium to high heat, grill your shrimp for one minute for one side, and the other minute in the center (3 minutes in total) or until it is bright pink and also cooked through. Then divide gazpacho into four bowls and then garnish with some grilled shrimp, cilantro leaves, diced avocado, and olive oil and then serve it immediately.

5.24 Grilled Blackened Salmon with Tomato, Avocado and Corn Salad

Prep time: 20 mins

Cooking time: 20 mins

Servings: 4

Ingredients:

- One and a half teaspoon of coriander
- Four five-ounce pieces of wild salmon
- One and a half teaspoon of brown sugar
- kosher salt
- One and a half teaspoon of chili powder
- Six tablespoons of olive oil
- Three tablespoons of red wine vinegar
- Half thinly sliced shallot
- Three corn ear
- A quarter cup of fresh cilantro, finely chopped
- A half-pint of halved yellow table tomatoes
- A half-pint of halved red grape tomatoes
- One and a half of diced avocados

- Freshly crushed black pepper

Instructions:

Heat grill to about medium to high and arrange skin-side down salmon on the plate. In a bowl, mix together brown sugar, coriander, and some chili powder and add some salt and then rub your mixture into the salmon. Place some wine vinegar and shallots in a small bowl and let it sit. Then, in a large bowl, mix together tomatoes, corn, cilantro and avocados. Heat three tablespoons of olive oil in a large ovenproof non-stick skillet on medium to high heat until it starts to smoke. Sear some skin-side-up salmon fillets for two minutes. Flip it, then shift skillet to the grill and then

cook for three minutes more, until salmon is cooked. Add shallots and wine vinegar to corn mixture sideways with three tablespoons of olive oil. Add some pepper and salt.

5.25 Grilled Sweet Pineapple Chili and Coconut Shrimp

Prep time: 10 mins

Cooking time: 10 mins

Servings: 4

Ingredients:

- Three tablespoons of coconut cream

- Two slices of ½ inch pineapple

- One teaspoon of sriracha

- Three tablespoons of chili sauce with pineapple sweet

- One pound of deveined and peeled shrimp

Instructions:

Mix everything for the sweet chili sauce of pineapple and coconut. For grilling shrimp, skewer shrimp and also pineapple and grill those over medium to high heat till cooked, about two to three minutes for each side. Onto your shrimp, brush sauce on it and enjoy.

5.26 Bbq Salmon with Mango Spicy and Sweet Salsa

Prep time: 10 mins

Cooking time: 15 mins

Servings: 4

Ingredients:

- One teaspoon of garlic powder
- Four 6-ounce of salmon fillets
- One teaspoon of chili powder
- juice of one lime
- Salt & pepper
- Two to three diced mangoes
- Half diced red pepper
- One small finely chopped and seeded jalapeño,
- 1/2 diced red onion
- A quarter cup of roughly chopped packed cilantro leaves

Instructions:

In a small bowl, mix together red peppers, mangos, jalapeños, onions, and cilantro. Put it to one side until it is ready to use. Mix together chili powder, garlic powder, and pepper and salt. Rub the mixture into the salmon fillets, then grill it over low to medium heat for about five to six minutes on every side. Squeeze some juice of fresh lime over grilled salmon and then top it with mango salsa.

5.27 Burrito Bowls of Fish Grilled Taco

Prep time: Half an hour

Cooking time: 35 mins

Servings: 4

Ingredients:

- Spray for non-stick
- Four 8- inch of flour tortillas, rounded
- Black pepper and salt
- One shallot
- Four fish filets
- Two garlic cloves
- Two tablespoons of olive oil
- One stemmed and seeded jalapeno
- One tablespoon of hot sauce
- One teaspoon of ground cumin
- One tablespoon of chili powder, chipotle
- Black pepper and salt
- 1 cup of diced strawberries
- One large diced, peeled and pitted mango
- One diced and pitted large peach
- 1/4 cup of red onion, diced
- One seeded, minced and stemmed jalapeno pepper
- A quarter cup of chopped cilantro
- Black pepper and salt
- One teaspoon of lime juice
- One cup of uncooked rice

- One tablespoon of fresh lime juice

- 1/4 cup of fresh cilantro

- One teaspoon of lime zest

- Four tortilla bowls

- Lime rice

- Chopped cilantro

- Four grilled fish filets

- Black pepper and salt

- Fruit salsa

- Two avocados crushed with black pepper and salt

- 4 cups of romaine lettuce, chopped

- Sour cream

Instructions:

For tortilla bowls, preheat the oven to about 400 degrees F. Take two to three oven bowls prepared and then place them on the downside on your baking sheet. If you have only two oven bowls, you

may need to do it in sets. Spray on each tortilla one side with non-stick spray, then sprinkle it with black pepper and salt, and place them side down on the bowls that are upside down. Press it to make around the bowl somewhat. They would not exactly stick but will start to take their shape and then place the tortillas into the oven and then bake for twelve and fifteen minutes or until it is crispy and brown. Remove it from heat, remove carefully the tortillas from your bowls. Set it aside, and then repeat if repetition is needed.

For grilled fish, in a bowl of the food processor, combine the garlic, shallot and jalapeno. Beat until the mixture is reduced to pulp. Then add your mixture to a shallow and large dish. Mix in the hot sauce, olive oil, cumin, chipotle chili powder, and black pepper and salt. Add to the dish the fish and flip it to coat. Let it marinate whilst you make the rest of the ingredients. Once it is marinated, heat your grill over medium to high heat. Then to the grill, add the fish and cook it for about three to four minutes on every side, or till it is cooked through. Remove it from heat and set it aside.

For fruit salsa, in a bowl, mix the strawberries, mango, red onion, peach, lime juice, cilantro and pepper and salt to taste. Toss it to combine and set it aside. For cilantro lime rice, prepare the rice by mixing lime zest cooked rice, lime juice, cilantro, and a pint of pepper and salt. Set it aside. To gather your bowls, with the lime rice, coat each bowl. Top it with fruit salsa, chopped lettuce, grilled fish, sour cream, avocado, and sprinkle it with fresh cilantro. Now, enjoy immediately.

Chapter 06: Recipes of Vegetables

All of the basic recipes for grilled vegetables, along with their particular ingredients and instructions, are discussed in detail and in-depth in this chapter. If you are a vegetarian and loves grilled food, you may find this chapter related to you. It will guide you to the best. It definitely consists of an infinite number of options to try according to your flavor.

6.1 Grilled Corn

Prep time: 5 mins

Cooking time: 10 mins

Servings: 4

Ingredients:

- Butter

- Four shucked ears corn

- Kosher salt

Instructions:

Preheat your grill to high and heat it for around 10 minutes. Same as with the grill pan and then add corn and cook for around 10 minutes until it turned charred. Now, spread butter over the warm corn and season it with salt. Serve your food immediately.

6.2 Grilled Asparagus

Prep time: 5 mins

Cooking time: 5 mins

Servings: 4

Ingredients:

- Kosher salt
- Two tablespoons olive oil extra-virgin
- 2 lb. stalks trimmed asparagus
- Ground black pepper

Instructions:

Heat your grill or the grill pan over a high flame. Roll your asparagus in oil and season with the pepper and salt. Grill asparagus until charred and tender for 3 to 4 minutes. Now, your grilled asparagus is ready to serve.

6.3 Green Grilled Beans

Prep time: 10 mins

Cooking time: 10 mins

Servings: 4

Ingredients:

- 1 lb. ends trimmed green beans
- Two tablespoon soy sauce
- Three tablespoon olive oil
- One tablespoon paste of chili garlic
- Red pepper flakes
- Two teaspoon honey
- Kosher salt
- Thinly sliced green onions

- Sesame seeds

- Chopped Roasted peanuts

Instructions:

Preheat your grill pan over medium-high heat. Stir together soy sauce, oil, honey, chili garlic paste and red pepper flakes in a bowl. Then add green beans and roll to coat. Season it with the salt. Now, put green beans on the grill pan and cook them for around 7 minutes. Garnish with green onions, sesame seeds and peanuts. Your food is ready to serve.

6.4 Grilled Potatoes

Prep time: 5 mins

Cooking time: 10 mins

Servings: 4-6

Ingredients:

- Two teaspoons of garlic powder

- 4 Russet potatoes, slice into wedges

- One teaspoon of kosher salt

- Half cup of extra-virgin olive oil

- One teaspoon black pepper, ground

- 2 tablespoons of herbs, chopped

Instructions:

Take a pot of water and bring it to a boil, then add potatoes and cook them for around 5 to 7 minutes. Drain potatoes and let them cool now; heat your grill to medium-high flame and oil grates. Stir together salt, garlic powder and pepper in a bowl with olive oil. Add potatoes and roll slightly to coat, then remove potatoes from the oil. Grill potatoes for around 5 minutes, turning one by one until golden brown. Add herbs to the remaining oil mixture, then return potatoes to the mixture and roll again.

6.5 Grilled Broccoli

Prep time: 5 mins

Cooking time: 10 mins

Servings: 6

Ingredients:

- 2 pounds of broccoli
- Two tablespoons of Worcestershire sauce
- ¼ cup of olive oil extra-virgin
- One tablespoon of soy sauce low-sodium
- One tablespoon of honey
- ¼ cup of freshly grated Parmesan
- Three cloves of grounded garlic
- Three tablespoons of ketchup
- ½ tablespoon of kosher salt
- ¼ tablespoon of crushed red pepper flakes, plus more for serving
- Freshly ground black pepper
- Lemon wedges, for the serving

Instructions:

Preheat your grill to medium heat. Trim off the bottom half of broccoli, then cut broccoli head into small trees. Stir together oil, Worcestershire, soy sauce, honey, ketchup, and garlic in a bowl. Season with pepper, salt, and red pepper flakes. Then, add in broccoli and roll to coat. Let sit for about 10 minutes. Put your broccoli on the grill and spray lightly with more salt. Now, it is the time to grill broccoli for around 8 to 10 minutes until tender and turning after every 2 minutes. Sprinkle with red pepper flakes and Parmesan, and serve with lemon wedges. Enjoy your food.

6.6 Bacon Cheddar Ranch Corn

Prep time: 5mins

Cooking time: 15 mins

Servings: 10

Ingredients:

- ½ cup of soft butter
- Chopped chives
- One packet ranch seasoning
- Freshly minced black pepper
- Ten ears corn
- 2 cups of shredded Cheddar
- Six slices of finely crumbled cooked bacon
- Ranch, for drizzling

Instructions:

Heat your grill to medium-high flame. Take a bowl and stir together butter, ranch seasoning and season with the pepper. Then, Rub ranch butter on corn and grill for 10 minutes until lightly charred. Top with cheddar and cover the grill for around 2 minutes to melt. Now, top with the cooked chives, bacon and drizzle with the ranch.

6.7 Grilled Artichoke

Prep time: 10 mins

Cooking time: 60 mins

Servings: 8

Ingredients:

- Four large artichokes
- 1/3 cups of olive oil extra-virgin
- One lemon

- Kosher salt

- Freshly ground black pepper

- ½ tablespoon of ground coriander

- 1 cup of raw pistachios

- ¼ cup of kosher salt

- Three garlic cloves, thinly sliced

- Two tablespoons of olive oil extra-virgin

- ¾ cups of plain Greek yogurt

- One tablespoon of lemon juice

- ¼ tablespoon of freshly ground black pepper

- One tablespoon of sesame seeds

- Lemon wedges, for serving

- ½ tablespoon of salt

- 1/2 c. finely chopped roasted pistachios

- chips of garlic, for garnish

Instructions:

Fill a stockpot with the water and squeeze in 1 lemon. By using kitchen equipment, trim off tips of the artichoke leaves and dipping cut areas into the lemon water one by one to prevent oxidation. Then, use a chef's knife to cut away the top of your artichoke. Peel off the outer tough leaves and use a knife or a peeler to remove the fibrous skin. Cut the artichoke in half and then remove the furry choke center by using a spoon. Rinse with the cold water and cleaning out the area surrounded by the choke. Put the cleaned artichokes into the lemon water and then clean the remaining artichokes.

Place a pot of artichokes over high heat and add a small amount of kosher salt, bring it to a boil. Now, lower the heat to medium and cook for about 15 minutes; cover the stems until stems are tender. Drain and let them cool. Heat the garlic and oil until the garlic turns golden. Remove heat immediately and spray salt on garlic chips.

In a food processor, process the pistachios and salt until finely ground, then add oil until smooth paste forms. Put it in another bowl and fold in lemon juice and yogurt.

In a skillet over medium flame, toast sesame, coriander, pepper, and salt for around 1 minute until fragrant or lightly golden. Put it in another small bowl and mix in salt, pistachios and pepper. Now, preheat your grill to medium heat and grease the artichokes with garlic oil and lightly season with salt and pepper. Serve your artichokes with a squeeze of lemon, a sprinkle of pistachio topping, a dollop of yogurt sauce and crushed garlic chips.

6.8 Campfire Popcorn

Prep time: 5 mins

Cooking time: 10 mins

Servings: 4

Ingredients:

- 1/4 tablespoon of garlic powder
- One tablespoon of vegetable oil
- 1/4 cup of popcorn kernels
- kosher salt

Instructions:

In a pie tin, combine popcorn kernels with vegetable oil. Cover firmly with foil and put on a campfire, doming the surface to provide space for the popcorn to pop. Carefully shake the pie tin with tongs until the popping ends. Season using garlic powder and salt.

6.9 Grilled Loaded Cauliflower

Prep time: 25 minutes

Cooking time: 20 minutes

Servings: 3-4

Ingredients:

- 1/2 tablespoon of garlic powder
- Two large heads of cauliflower
- 1/4 cup of olive oil extra-virgin

- 1/2 tablespoon of paprika

- Freshly ground black pepper

- 2 cups of shredded cheddar

- Kosher salt

- Two tablespoons of finely chopped chives

- Ranch dressing for drizzling

- Eight slices of cooked bacon, crumbled

Instructions:

Remove the leaves of each head of cauliflower and dispose of them, then cut the stem such that the cauliflower may lay flat on the chopping board. Slice each cauliflower head into 3/4" thick "steaks." Some loose florets should be set aside to prepare along with the steaks. Whisk together garlic powder, paprika, olive oil in a tiny cup. Season using pepper and salt to taste. Preheat a grill pan or grill to moderate temperature. Brush each steak's one side using the olive oil mixture and put it on the grill with the oil side down. Brush the top surfaces using the olive oil blend and cook for around 8 minutes on each side or until soft and crispy in spots on both sides. Top cauliflower using cheese and cook until it has melted. Toss any leftover florets in the mixture of olive oil and grill for around 6 minutes, rotating often until crispy and juicy. Drizzle ranch dressing over the cauliflower, and finish with cooked bacon plus chives.

6.10 Campfire Potatoes

Prep time: 10 mins

Cooking time: 20 mins

Servings: 4

Ingredients:

- One tablespoon of garlic powder

- 2 pounds of mini Yukon Gold potatoes, quartered

- Two tablespoons of olive oil

- Kosher salt

- Freshly ground black pepper

- 2 cups of shredded mozzarella

- 1 cup of freshly grated Parmesan

- Chopped fresh parsley for garnish

- One tablespoon of dried oregano

- Crushed red pepper flakes for garnish

Instructions:

Preheat the grill to moderate temperature. Cut four 10-inch-long strips of foil. Mix potatoes with garlic powder, oregano and olive oil in a big bowl and season using pepper and salt.

Roll the foil packets sideways to fully cover the potatoes after dividing the potatoes among the foil pieces. To secure the upper and bottom corners, roll them. Position foil packets on grill and grill for around 15 minutes, or until nearly cooked through. Unpack the foil packages and top the potatoes with Parmesan and mozzarella. Fold the foil again over the vegetable and grill for another 5 minutes, or until the cheese melts. Serve warm, garnished with parsley plus red flakes.

6.11 Grilled Brussels Sprouts

Prep time: 15 mins

Cooking time: 15 mins

Servings: 6

Ingredients:

- Three tablespoons of olive oil type extra-virgin

- 1/4 cup of balsamic vinegar

- 1 ounce of brussels sprouts, halved

- One tablespoon of grainy mustard

- Two tablespoons of crushed red pepper flakes

- One tablespoon honey

- Kosher salt

- 1/2 cup of freshly grated Parmesan for garnish

Instructions:

Preheat the grill to a high temperature. Combine the olive oil, Brussels sprouts, vinegar, mustard, pepper flakes and honey in a big mixing bowl and season using salt. Thread sprouts onto skewers made of metal. Grill for around 10 minutes, rotating regularly until sprouts are soft and grilled through. Before eating, brush with Parmesan cheese.

6.12 Bang Bang Corn

Prep time: 10 mins

Cooking time: 14 mins

Servings: 4

Ingredients:

- Three tablespoons of melted butter
- Juice of 2 limes
- One tablespoon of sriracha
- 1/2 cup of sweet chili sauce
- Two finely minced cloves of garlic
- Freshly ground black pepper
- Six ears corn, husks removed
- kosher salt
- Freshly chopped cilantro for garnish

Instructions:

To make bang butter, blend butter, chili sauce, garlic, lime juice and Sriracha in a medium-sized bowl and season using pepper and salt generously. Using a pastry brush, slather butter on the corn. Preheat the grill to moderate temperature. Grill corn for around 15 minutes, rotating and drip with the rest of bang-bang butter regularly, until crispy and charred. Serve with cilantro garnished on top.

6.13 Grilled Corn Salsa

Prep time: 15 mins

Cooking time: 15 mins

Servings: 6

Ingredients:

- Kosher salt

- Five ears of yellow corn, husks removed

- Two tablespoons of olive oil

- 1 cup of quartered grape tomatoes

- 1/2 red onion that is finely chopped

- One ripe chopped avocado

- One tablespoon of crushed red pepper flakes

- Two tablespoons of sliced basil

- 1/3 cup of lime juice

- One minced clove of garlic

Instructions:

Season corn using salt and brush it with the oil. Grill for around 8 minutes, or just as the kernels start to char. Allow it to cool a bit before slicing the kernels with a knife off the corn. Combine avocado, corn, tomatoes, basil and onion in a wide bowl. Combine the oil, garlic, pepper flakes and lime in a medium-sized bowl. Season using salt, then whisk until soft. Pour the paste over the salsa and whisk until it is well combined. Eat alongside tortilla chips on the plate

6.14 Cauliflower Grilled Cheese

Prep time: 25 mins

Cooking time: 20 mins

Servings: 3-4

Ingredients:

- 1 1/2 cup of shredded white Cheddar

- Two lightly beaten eggs

- 1/2 cup of finely grated Parmesan

- One head of cauliflower to make about 4 cups processed cauliflower

- 1/2 tablespoon of oregano

Instructions:

Cauliflower should be cut into florets. In a food blender, pulse cauliflower florets until they imitate rice. Likewise, the cauliflower can be grated. Combine the processed cauliflower, Parmesan, oregano and eggs in a medium-sized bowl. Mix until thoroughly combined, and use pepper and salt to season. Over moderate flame, heat a broad nonstick skillet. Spray the pan using cooking spray, then pour the cauliflower mixture on the pan's one side into a small patty. Shape a new patty on the opposite hand. Cook for around 5 minutes, pushing down on both patties using a spatula until golden underneath. Cook for another 3 minutes on the other side or until golden. Place cheese on one cauliflower slice, then the next cauliflower slice on top of it. Cook for another 2 minutes a side, just until the cheese has melted. Repeat for the rest of the ingredients.

6.15 Grilled Ranch Potatoes

Prep time: 5 mins

Cooking time: 15 mins

Servings: 8

Ingredients:

- 1/4 tablespoon of olive oil type extra-virgin

- Two halved baby potatoes

- Juice of 1/2 a lemon

- 1/2 packet of ranch seasoning

- kosher salt

- Ranch dressing for drizzling

- Freshly ground black pepper

- Chopped fresh chives for garnish

Instructions:

Preheat the grill to moderate temperature. Mix potatoes with lemon juice, ranch seasoning and olive oil in a big bowl. Season using pepper and salt according to taste. Hook potatoes on skewers and cook for around 15 minutes, or until juicy and mildly charred. Garnish using chives and drizzle ranch dressing over them.

6.16 Spicy and Sweet Grilled Corn

Prep time: 5 mins

Cooking time: 10 mins

Servings: 6

Ingredients:

- Three tablespoons of packed brown sugar

- 1/4 cup of melted butter

- One tablespoon of cayenne pepper

- Six ears corn, husked

- kosher salt

- Freshly ground black pepper

- Lime wedges, for squeezing

Instructions:

Preheat the grill to a high temperature. Brush grates using oil and add the corn. Grill for around 5 minutes, rotating once. In the meantime, mix brown sugar, salt, cayenne, butter and pepper in a medium-sized bowl. Whisk everything together, so it's smooth. When the corn is grilling, baste it with crack sauce until it is fully covered. Grill for another 5 minutes until tender and charred. Serve with lime juice squeezed on top.

6.17 Grilled Zucchini

Prep time: 5 mins

Cooking time: 5 mins

Servings: 2

Ingredients:

- Two thick strips sliced medium zucchini
- One tablespoon of olive oil, which is extra-virgin
- Half teaspoon of lemon zest
- ¼ teaspoon of crushed red pepper and some more for garnishing
- Kosher salt
- Freshly crushed black pepper
- Four torn basil leaves

Instructions:

Heat the grill on medium to high. In a big bowl with lemon zest, oil, and flakes of red pepper, toss zucchini. Season it with pepper and salt. Once the grill is hot, sensibly use pincers to rub a paper towel with oil over grates. Using forceps, position zucchini on the grill and cover and then cook for about 3 minutes. Then flip and continue to cook on high, 2 to 3 minutes more, covered. When zucchini is delicate, remove it from heat and then garnish it with red pepper and basil.

6.18 Romaine Grilled Caesar Wedge

Prep time: 10 mins

Cooking time: 10 mins

Servings: 4

Ingredients:

- 3/4 cup of mayonnaise

- One teaspoon of honey mustard

- One clove of minced garlic

- One teaspoon of Worcestershire sauce

- kosher salt

- Juice of a half lemon

- 3/4 cup of halved grape tomatoes

- Freshly crushed black pepper

- Two tablespoons of olive oil which is extra-virgin

- One large quartered romaine head lettuce

- Four slices of chopped and cooked bacon

Instructions:

For making creamy Caesar dressing, in a small bowl, mix together garlic, mayo, Worcestershire, honey mustard, and lemon juice and then season with pepper and salt. Set it aside. Heat grill pan over medium to high heat. With olive oil, brush the romaine wedges and grill it until charred and then for 2 to 3 minutes per side slightly wilted. Transfer the romaine to a plate and then drizzle it with dressing. Top it with tomatoes and bacon, and then serve.

6.19 Cauliflower and Zucchini Skewers Style Feta

Prep time: 10 mins

Cooking time: 10 mins

Servings: 8

Ingredients:

- Four summer squash and large zucchini

- One cut head cauliflower

- Eight skewers which are soaked in water for about 20 minutes

- Olive oil, which is extra-virgin, for drizzling

- kosher salt

- Freshly crushed black pepper

- 1/4 cup crumbled feta

Instructions:

Preheat your grill to about medium to high. Shave the yellow squash and zucchini into long strips with the use of a Y peeler. Skewer yellow squash, zucchini, and cauliflower, then drizzle with some olive oil and season it with peppers and alt. Grill it, turning frequently, until vegetables are slightly charred and tender, about 10 to 12 minutes. Crumble it with feta.

6.20 Mexican Street Style Corn

Prep time: 5 mins

Cooking time: 20 mins

Servings: 4

Ingredients:

- Six cleaned and shucked ears corn

- 1/2 cup of mayonnaise

- Chili powder

- 1/3 cup of Grated cotija cheese

- Freshly sliced cilantro

- Lime wedges

Instructions:

Preheat your grill or grill pan to about medium to high. Grill the corn, often turning, until somewhat charred all over for about 10 minutes. Brush your corn with a mayonnaise layer and sprinkle it onto it with cotija, chili powder, and cilantro. Then, serve warm with some lime wedges.

6.21 Grilled Mix Vegetables

Prep time: 8 mins

Cooking time: 12 mins

Servings: 6

Ingredients:

- One pound of bell peppers

- One pound of zucchini

- One large white or red onion is cut into thick half-inch rounds

- Cooking spray

- One-third cup of Italian basil or parsley, which is finely chopped

- Two tablespoons of extra virgin olive oil

- Ground black pepper

- Two cloves of garlic which are grated

- Two tablespoons of balsamic vinegar

- One teaspoon of salt

Instructions:

In a medium or small bowl, mix together balsamic vinegar, olive oil, garlic, pepper and salt. Set it aside. Preheat your grill on medium heat and spray it with a spray of cooking. Position vegetables in one layer on your grill, then close the cover and heat for 12 minutes, once flipping. Vegetables should be gentle to the touch, with nice marks on the grill. Cook for a longer time if you want soft vegetables. Transfer these vegetables to a bowl, then on the top pour balsamic dressing, then sprinkle with basil/parsley and then gently mix. Serve cold, warm or hot with seafood or grilled meat and brown rice or a side of quinoa.

6.22 Grilled Peppers having Cheese

Prep time: 15 mins

Cooking time: 10 mins

Servings: 12

Ingredients:

- Eight mini peppers sliced and seeded in half
- Six ounces of goat cheese
- Grapeseed oil or olive oil for peppers brushing
- Six ounces of light cream cheese
- Half tablespoon of fresh juice of a lemon
- Two tablespoons of finely chopped fresh chives
- Two teaspoons of minced garlic
- Two tablespoons of finely chopped fresh parsley
- Pepper and salt to taste

Instructions:

To make peppers, preheat your grill to medium-high heat. Brush the peppers' skins with grapeseed oil or olive oil and set it on a platter. Grill these peppers over low to medium heat for five to seven minutes or till the skin, is somewhat blistered. Remove them from the grill. To make the filling, mix herbs and cheeses together when it is fluffy and light, then mix in juice of lemon, season with pepper and salt. Spoon the filling into peppers which are grilled, and garnish them with fresh chives. Serve immediately.

6.23 Garlic Balsamic Grilled Skewers in Mushroom Style

Prep time: Half an hour

Cooking time: 10 min

Servings: 4

Ingredients:

- Two tablespoons of balsamic vinegar

- Two pounds of sliced mushrooms which are 1/4 inch thick

- Two tablespoons of soy sauce

- Half teaspoon of chopped thyme

- Three cloves of chopped garlic

- Pepper and salt to taste

Instructions:

Marinate in the combination of the other ingredients in the mushrooms for about 30 minutes. Skewer your mushrooms and then grill over medium heat until it is tender and somewhat charred, about two to three minutes on each side.

6.24 Grilled Asparagus, Mushroom and Salad of Wild Rice with Feta

Prep time: 10 mins

Cooking time: 50 mins

Servings: 4

Ingredients:

- Half cup of wild rice

- One tablespoon of oil

- One-quarter cups of broth, vegetable or chicken

- One diced onion

- 8 ounces of mushrooms, sliced and cleaned

- Two chopped cloves of garlic

- pepper and salt to taste

- One pound of asparagus, cut and trimmed into pieces of bite-sized

- 1 tablespoon of oil

- Two tablespoons chopped dill

- Four cups of salad greens

- A quarter cup of balsamic vinaigrette

- A quarter cup of goat cheese or feta or crumbled blue cheese

Instructions:

Boil broth and white rice, then decrease to low heat and cover for around 50 minutes, or until the rice become soft. Warm the oil in a frying pan for around 30 minutes. Add onion and cook, stirring occasionally, until the onion is soft, around 3-5 minutes. Sauté the garlic for around a minute, or until fragrant. Season using pepper and salt to taste after adding the mushrooms and sauté until only caramelized around 10-15 minutes. In the meantime, mix the asparagus with pepper and salt to taste the oil. Arrange the asparagus in one layer on a dish and grill until tender, around 10-15 minutes, by placing it on the grill. Combine the mushrooms, wild rice, asparagus, balsamic

vinaigrette and dill in a large mixing bowl. Serve on a layer of salad greens along with the wild rice and mushrooms, finished with grilled asparagus and crushed feta.

6.25 Balsamic Grilled Soy Garlic Mushrooms

Prep time: 5 minutes

Cooking time: 20 minutes

Servings: 4

Ingredients:

- Two pounds of mushrooms

- Three tablespoons of balsamic vinegar

- One tablespoon of oil

- Two tablespoons of soy sauce

- 1/2 chopped teaspoon thyme, or a quarter teaspoon of dried thyme)

- Three chopped cloves of garlic

- Pepper and salt to taste

Instructions:

Add the mushrooms to the balsamic vinegar, oil, soy sauce, thyme, garlic, pepper and salt, then place in one layer on grill and grill for around 20 minutes, dripping mixture midway through.

COOKING CONVERSION CHART

Measurement

CUP	ONCES	MILLILITERS	TABLESPOONS
8 cup	64 oz	1895 ml	128
6 cup	48 oz	1420 ml	96
5 cup	40 oz	1180 ml	80
4 cup	32 oz	960 ml	64
2 cup	16 oz	480 ml	32
1 cup	8 oz	240 ml	16
3/4 cup	6 oz	177 ml	12
2/3 cup	5 oz	158 ml	11
1/2 cup	4 oz	118 ml	8
3/8 cup	3 oz	90 ml	6
1/3 cup	2.5 oz	79 ml	5.5
1/4 cup	2 oz	59 ml	4
1/8 cup	1 oz	30 ml	3
1/16 cup	1/2 oz	15 ml	1

Temperature

FAHRENHEIT	CELSIUS
100 °F	37 °C
150 °F	65 °C
200 °F	93 °C
250 °F	121 °C
300 °F	150 °C
325 °F	160 °C
350 °F	180 °C
375 °F	190 °C
400 °F	200 °C
425 °F	220 °C
450 °F	230 °C
500 °F	260 °C
525 °F	274 °C
550 °F	288 °C

Weight

IMPERIAL	METRIC
1/2 oz	15 g
1 oz	29 g
2 oz	57 g
3 oz	85 g
4 oz	113 g
5 oz	141 g
6 oz	170 g
8 oz	227 g
10 oz	283 g
12 oz	340 g
13 oz	369 g
14 oz	397 g
15 oz	425 g
1 lb	453 g

Conclusion:

Grilling is a form of dry-heat cooking that relies on heat transfer by the air from the open flame. On the exterior of the food, browning reactions are induced by this method of cooking, which promotes the production of complex aromas and flavors. Grilling is a nice way to spend the summer. Favorite vegetables and meat only tend to taste good when prepared outside. Grilling, on the other side, is not just for holidays and backyard pleasure. Grilled foods provide a number of health advantages that aren't possible from other cooking techniques. Less fat is among the most important health effects of grilling. Excess fat from inside foods spills away until ever touching the plate, needing less fat to grill vegetables and meat to perfection. For extra taste and convenience of cooking, throw grilled veggies in some good olive oil, and a thin coating of spray for cooking can prevent most food from sticking. Grilled foods are prepared using a source of heat that is not specifically under the product. This encourages thick food products to be cooked steadily, which is important to prevent the food from burning on the outside until the internal part achieves the required doneness. Foods including entire turkeys, pork roasts, beef roasts, and chickens are excellent candidates for indirect grilling.

Grilling with indirect heat is commonly used in combination with heat grilling, which is direct. Large cuts of beef may be burnt straight over a high flame to lock in the juices and keep the meat tender. The meat is then put on a section of the grilling plate that is aside from the heat source, allowing the indirect heat to steadily cook the meat before it is cooked. The heat supply for grilling is from below. Due to the great taste it imparts to food, grilling is among the most common cooking techniques. When the juice rich in nutrients drips from the meat during grilling, though, up to 40 percent of B vitamins can be lost. Polycyclic aromatic hydrocarbons known as PAHs, which are cancer-causing compounds possibly formed as meat is being grilled and the fat spills onto a hot surface, are often a source of concern. If drippings are eliminated and smoke is decreased, researchers discovered that PAHs might be reduced by 41–89%. Grilling adds a lot of spice, but it also decreases vitamin B. Grilling often produces chemicals that can cause cancer. Grilling will improve your mood as well as your physical health. In the summer, grilling is a common social activity that allows people to entertain their guests. When tending to the grill, sitting outdoors with friends allows for opportunities for interaction and togetherness, which is good for both the mind and body.

Printed in Great Britain
by Amazon